Baptist Men in Missions

A Guide for Organizing and Operating a Baptist Men's Unit

BY CLYDE L. DAVIS
Consultant, Brotherhood Administration
Brotherhood Commission, SBC

Code Number: **Church Study Course**
This book is number 6602 of the Christian Leadership Series

Library of Congress catalog card number: 75-101630
Printed in the United States of America

Contents

Acknowledgments

● No book is the product of one person. Concepts grow out of many contacts with persons who express their thoughts about the subject. Facts are obtained from sources which record the fruits of many lifetimes of research. Methods are structured from crushed efforts of many leaders who dared to try new approaches.

Hundreds of people have influenced this book. Many volunteer Brotherhood workers in churches, associations, and state conventions contributed to the formulation of a concept of need around which this book was planned. The staff of the Brotherhood Commission and Brotherhood directors in the state Baptist conventions provided technical assistance through their constructive criticism of the manuscript. For all of their assistance the author is grateful.

Much of the material in this book reflects concepts and methods contained in *Missionary Education for Baptist Men* by George L. Euting and *Missionary Education for Baptist Young Men* by Norman Godfrey. The author is grateful to both of these men.

A special word of gratitude goes to Mrs. Joan Byrd for her patience in typing this manuscript.

About the Author

● Clyde L. Davis has been in Brotherhood work since 1931, the year he became Ambassador-in-chief of the Royal Ambassador chapter in his home church at Natalbany, Louisiana. Since that day he has held various leadership positions in work with men and boys.

Born in Kentwood, Louisiana in 1920, he was reared in southeastern Louisiana. Beginning in December, 1938 he served nearly seven years in the United States Navy. His free time on and off the ship was given to service through various Christian movements witnessing to service men.

Discharged from the Navy in 1945, Mr. Davis attended Clarke Memorial College at Newton, Mississippi and Mississippi College at Clinton, Mississippi, where he received his bachelor of arts degree in 1951. In 1957 he received his bachelor of divinity degree from Southeastern Baptist Theological Seminary, Wake Forest, North Carolina.

As a college student, Mr. Davis was pastor of several churches in Mississippi. While attending the seminary he was pastor of West Side Baptist Church at Red Springs, North Carolina. This church had two Brotherhoods (Baptist Men's units). He was associational Brotherhood president in Robeson association (North Carolina).

As regional Brotherhood president he represented the North Carolina Brotherhood department in nine associations. In 1957 he became superintendent of missions for New South River Association.

Mr. Davis began his career as a professional Brotherhood worker in 1959 as secretary of the Brotherhood Department for the Baptist State Convention of North Carolina, a post he held for almost seven years. In 1966 he joined the Brotherhood Commission at Memphis, Tennessee as secretary of the Men's Department. Since then he has served in field services as supervisor of men's work and more recently as Brotherhood administration consultant.

Mr. Davis married the former Thelma Haman of Lumberton, North Carolina. They have four children, Clyde Jr., William Earl, David, and Mary Elaine.

Foreword

● Baptist Men is the adult division of Brotherhood. The church uses its Baptist Men's units to teach missions to men, to involve them in mission action designed to witness and minister to persons of special need and circumstance, to support world missions through prayer and giving, and to provide leadership for special projects.

Baptist Men's units hold tremendous possibilities in any church, regardless of size or location. Properly functioning, the organization, regardless of size, can be instrumental in meeting human need in areas of life that demands the attention and message of the church. This organization in reality is a bridge builder. It enables the church to effectively utilize men in moving from its building into the avenues of life where the action is. A church needs Baptist Men's units to perform at its maximum. Baptist Men uniquely strengthens a church's ministry and witness.

Persons chosen to lead in Baptist Men or participate in its activities need to understand the basic purpose of the organization and how it functions. The purpose of this book is to provide this information.

Included in this book are suggestions on possible organizational patterns designed to enable any church, regardless of size, to provide mission education for men and involve them in purposeful and meaningful mission activities. With the patterns of organization is information on the duties of officers, scope of work to be performed, relationships with other church organizations, curriculum materials and organizational aids available, and other general information about Baptist Men's work.

Officers and members of Baptist Men need to read this book.

GEORGE W. SCHROEDER
Executive Secretary
Brotherhood Commission
Southern Baptist Convention

Introduction

- "The challenge of overseas mission continues, as does the home missionary challenge. Both of the mission boards of the Southern Baptist Convention have broadened their work to include more and more laymen as short-term or career missionaries.

"Of equal importance is the recognition that we confront a missionary frontier on every hand. Our churches in America are surrounded by a society that is pagan for the most part.

"On the one hand, our churches have largely conformed to this non-Christian culture. Too often they accept worldly standards of success. Too often they merely reflect the cultural, economic, and class structure of the non-Christian world, distinctions that are supposedly done away in the reconciling work of Christ. Our churches themselves are mission fields in need of evangelizing. . . .

"If the churches are too conformed to the secular world, they are also too separated from it. They live their in-group life, sending a few missionaries to far places but not engaging the real world around them in vital contact. Nothing is so much needed as the transformation of our churches into missions, into cells of God's people who pioneer in the secular frontier which meets them at every turn.

"Here is a new missionary challenge for men. In addition to the missionaries who go to frontiers, there is the call for men to give their witness in every area of the secular life which surrounds us. Women will aid and are aiding in the pioneering witness, but courageous Christian men must penetrate the secular occupations with the Christian gospel. Christ's men must venture into the riot-torn inner cities. They must stand their ground and refuse to desert the asphalt jungles for the security of the suburbs. Men must speak and live the gospel on the frontiers of racial strife and turmoil.

"This is a call for men to turn the church inside out and direct it into the all pervasive pagan culture. Wherever people are isolated and alienated from the church in urban ghetto or highrise apartment, in juvenile gangs, or agnostic intelligentsia, these men must be present to represent Christ and his gospel.

"All of the daring of Spirit-filled men with their aggressive, pioneering drive is needed to face the tough, non-Christian world at our doorsteps.

"All of the inventive genius of men is required to chart new courses for the Christian witness in American paganism. And all of the hardheaded realism of men is called for to keep us from idealistic woolgathering.

"What would happen if the concerned men in your church—not to exclude the women, of course—were to meet together for earnest prayer, seek the wisdom and empowering of the Holy Spirit, and proceed to analyze the needs for mission and ministry in your community? Then, most important of all what if these Spirit-filled men were to launch out on missions, no holds barred, no color or class lines recognized, and no job too difficult to tackle?" [1]

One of the most vital movements within churches in recent years has been the involvement of men in the mission work of their church. No longer do men sit back while women carry the load of mission education. Men are demonstrating a genuine interest in learning and being involved in the church's mission work.

The rise of a new appreciation for the church's mission program has accompanied this new enthusiasm. More of the biblical meaning of the church has taken the place of the organization and institutional interpretation. This has brought about a new appreciation for the church as a channel

---

[1] Luther Copeland, "Masculinity in Missions," *Home Life* (Sunday School Board, SBC, Nashville, Tennessee, July, 1968), p. 17.

for expression of the spirit of Christ in the world today. Learning what is the true mission of the church and how to become involved in it has become a real concern of men.

This book is written to interpret the procedures for putting this interest and enthusiasm to work for Christ. It brings together the insight of many leaders who have influenced the evolution of Baptist Men's work. It applies these insights to the duties, relationships, and attitudes of the officers to assist them in becoming effective leaders representing in thought and deed the spirit of Christ.

Information in each chapter relates to a specific area of Baptist Men's work. There are some instances of purposeful repetition. Nevertheless, each chapter is so related to a specific area of work or position of responsibility that each officer will find the major part of his duties described in one chapter. All officers, however, should read and understand the entire book.

This book was written with a Baptist men's unit in mind. Except for the suggestions for grouping men in Chapter I, discussion is limited to the work of a single unit. That unit may be composed of only Baptist Young Men, Baptist Men, or Senior Baptist Men, or a combination of the three groups.

No effort was made to suggest ways for adapting methods to various age-levels or for coordinating the work of multiple units. Coordination of work for multiple units is done by the Brotherhood council. Guidance for this action is *Brotherhood Program of a Baptist Church.*

1. Beginning Baptist Men's Work

CHAPTER OUTLINE

A. DEFINITIONS
1. BAPTIST MEN
2. BAPTIST MEN'S UNIT
3. PROGRAM
4. MISSION PROGRAM
5. TASK
6. MISSION STUDY
7. MISSION ACTION
8. PROJECT

B. OBJECTIVE

C. TASKS
1. TEACH MISSIONS
2. ENGAGE IN MISSION ACTION
3. SUPPORT WORLD MISSIONS THROUGH PRAYING AND GIVING
4. PROVIDE AND INTERPRET INFORMATION REGARDING THE WORK OF THE CHURCH AND DENOMINATION

D. RELATIONSHIPS
1. THE CHURCH AND ITS PROGRAM OF WORK
2. THE ASSOCIATIONAL BROTHERHOOD

E. ORGANIZATION
1. GROUPING BAPTIST MEN
2. UNIT ORGANIZATION
3. DUTIES OF OFFICERS

F. STEPS FOR BEGINNING
1. DETERMINE ORGANIZATION
2. CHOOSE OFFICERS
3. TRAIN OFFICERS
4. BEGIN PLANNING
5. PUBLICIZE MEETING
6. CONDUCT UNIT MEETING

● The purpose of this chapter is to provide basic concepts of Baptist Men's work and help in organizing units. Basic to concept are definitions, relationships, organizational patterns, and an outline of officers' duties.

A. DEFINITIONS

1. BAPTIST MEN

Baptist Men is the adult division of Brotherhood which involves men in a church's mission program.

2. BAPTIST MEN'S UNIT

A Baptist Men's unit is an organized group of men within the adult division of Brotherhood. A church may have several units based on age-levels or the time of day and week groups of men can meet.

3. PROGRAM

A group of closely related basic continuing activities of primary importance (tasks) in achieving an objective.

4. MISSION PROGRAM

A mission program is that part of the church's program which majors upon the interpretation and application of the missionary message of the Bible.

5. TASK

A task is a basic continuing activity of primary importance in achieving an objective.

6. MISSION STUDY

Mission study is that part of a mission program which helps persons increase their knowledge and understanding of missions and motivates them to become personally involved in missions.

7. MISSION ACTION

Mission action is the organized effort of a church to minister and witness to persons of special need or circumstance who, without this special effort, are often bypassed in the church's direct outreach activities.

8. PROJECT

A project is a church activity that has a recognized beginning and ending. Although a project may be repeated from time to time, it is not considered continuous.

B. OBJECTIVE

The objective of Baptist Men is to assist the church in its task of leading men to a deeper commitment to missions, to a more meaningful prayer life for missions, to a larger stewardship on behalf of missions, and to a personal involvement in missions.

C. TASKS

A Baptist Men's unit is guided in its work by four Brotherhood tasks. Tasks indicate the areas of work normally assigned to Brotherhood by a church. Introduced here, the four tasks are discussed in more detail in Chapters III-V.

1. TEACH MISSIONS

To teach missions means to lead men to develop new concepts, understandings, and appreciation of the total mission of the church; to develop new attitudes about the mission of the church and the persons not now enrolled in its programs; and to develop new skills through taking part in the church's mission. Content includes the missionary message of the Bible; role of the church in missions, progress of Christian missions, and contemporary missions.

2. ENGAGE IN MISSION ACTION

The purpose of this task is to lead men to become personally involved in ministering and witnessing to persons of special need or circumstance who would otherwise be bypassed by the church's direct outreach effort.

3. SUPPORT WORLD MISSIONS THROUGH PRAYING AND GIVING

The purpose of this task is to lead men to pray for missionaries and mission needs and to support financially the mission work of their church and denomination.

4. PROVIDE AND INTERPRET INFORMATION REGARDING THE WORK OF THE CHURCH AND DENOMINATION

This task is common to all church program organizations such as Sunday School, Training Union, Woman's Missionary Union, Music Ministry or Brotherhood. The church and denomination uses the various curriculum materials and activities of the program organizations to communicate information to members of the church and its organizations.

D. RELATIONSHIPS

A Baptist Men's unit does not exist unto itself. It is part of Brotherhood which is a church program organization. A thorough understanding of a Baptist Men's unit's relationship to the church and its programs of work and the associational Brotherhood is essential.

1. THE CHURCH AND ITS PROGRAMS OF WORK

a. *The Church*

A Baptist Men's unit performs work (tasks) assigned to it by the church. The actions a unit proposes for doing this work and the results are communicated through the Brotherhood council to the church council for evaluation and coordination.

b. *The Brotherhood Council*

As a member of the Brotherhood council, the president represents the Baptist Men's unit in planning, coordinating, and evaluating Brotherhood work. He receives assignments for the unit, reports on plans, proposes actions initiated by the unit, and makes requests for unit needs.

Other leaders in the unit may be asked to meet with the Brotherhood council to discuss proposed actions which involve detailed planning in their area of work.

c. *Royal Ambassadors*

Even though the Royal Ambassador organization is separate from Baptist Men, both are part of Brotherhood and therefore share common tasks. They relate to each other through the Brotherhood council. Baptist Men's units should be responsive to requests for help the Royal Ambassador Leader may make such as men to serve on the Royal Ambassador committee, counselors, or help with sports, camping, and transportation.

d. *Other Church Programs*

A Baptist Men's unit seeks with other church programs to provide mutual assistance in accomplishing church tasks. For example, Training Union may provide time and teachers for training officers, or a unit may jointly sponsor a mission action with Baptist Women. A Baptist Men's unit also may give help to church programs such as evangelism and stewardship. It's usually through projects at the request of the church.

2. THE ASSOCIATIONAL BROTHERHOOD

The association exists to assist churches. The associational Brotherhood is an organization of the association created to help churches establish, conduct, enlarge and improve their Brotherhood work.

The Baptist Men's president of the associational Brotherhood is responsible for helping Baptist Men's units in the churches. He provides training opportunities, program information and interpretation, and personal help to the units.

The president of a Baptist Men's unit should keep abreast of all services available from the association. He may want to offer to help the associational Baptist Men's president assist other churches.

E. ORGANIZATION

Organization is a mechanism or structure which enables people to work together effectively. It is a process of identifying and grouping the work to be performed, defining and assigning responsibility and authority, and establishing relationships to enable people to work together effectively in accomplishing objectives. Organization is a means to an end.

Using the guidelines on grouping and organization which follow, any church regardless of size can have the organization it needs to motivate and involve men in missions.

1. GROUPING BAPTIST MEN

A church may have as many Baptist Men's units as it needs for involving a maximum number of men in missions. The number of units a church has should be influenced by three factors: (1) number of men available, (2) age-levels of men within the church membership, and (3) the work schedules of men. The types of units a church decides to have is referred to as the grouping plan.

Three basic grouping plans which incorporate the factors above are suggested for a church to consider. When deciding on the number and types of units, a church shouldn't take an either/or view of the grouping plans, but select among the parts for the best combination. For example, a church may have three Baptist Men's units based on the age-level factor (18-29, 30-59, and 60-up) meeting at night, and another unit (18-up) based on the work schedule factor which meets in a downtown restaurant during the lunch hour. However, a small church with a limited number of men may have only one unit for all men 18 and older and meet at a time convenient to most of the men. Here are some examples of grouping plans.

a. *Grouping for Small Number of Men*

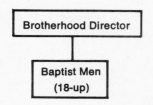

Grouping for Small Number of Men

b. *Grouping by Age-Levels*

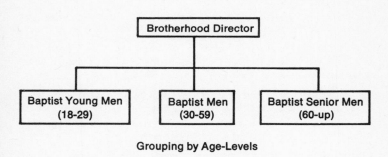

Grouping by Age-Levels

Grouping to accommodate men's work schedules is particularly suited to churches having men who work on different shifts or men whose work requires them to travel out of town during the week. For example, Unit 1 may meet for lunch in one section of a city where the men get off at the same time. Unit 2 may have night meetings at the church. Unit 3 may have a breakfast meeting during the week or on the week-end. Times for meetings should harmonize with the men's work schedules.

2. Unit Organization

a. *Organizational Patterns*

The number of officers in a unit is determined by the number of men and capable leaders in the unit. The various combinations of officers in a unit are called organizational patterns.

Before choosing an organizational pattern, persons beginning a unit should answer two questions: (1) How many men are available for this unit? (2) How many men within this group are capable leaders? The answers to these questions will help determine the number of officers a unit will have.

A small number of men in a unit means a light work load in each area of responsibility and makes it possible to combine two or more areas of responsibility into one office.

Possible combinations of officers according to size of a unit and number of available leaders are:

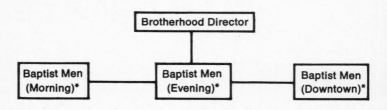

Grouping to Accommodate Men's Work Schedule
*Examples of Variations

The president assumes responsibility for leading all areas of work for the unit in Pattern I.

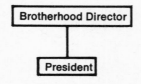

Pattern I — 5-10 Members and One Leader

In Pattern II the president performs the duties normally assigned to him, plus the duties of the vice-president and secretary.

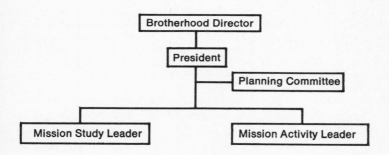

Pattern II — 10-20 Members and Three Leaders

Pattern III is the basic organizational plan for a Baptist Men's unit. It allows for equal distribution of leadership responsibilities.

This principle of flexibility may apply in churches having only one Baptist Men's unit or in churches having multiple units. A church may have five officers in one Baptist Men's unit and one to three officers in another.

b. *Adding Working Groups*

Additional organizational needs can be met by adding working groups under the Mission Study Leader and the Mission Activity Leader. Here is an example:

23

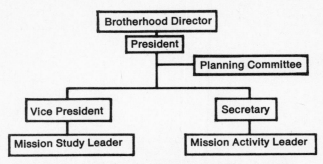

Pattern III — More Than 20 Members and Five Leaders

Working groups are formed by the Mission Study Leader or the Mission Activity Leader in conference with the president when the unit has a specific task a small group can do well. The group leader and group members are appointed by the Mission Study Leader or Mission Activity Leader with approval of the president.

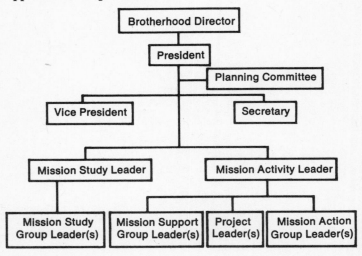

3. DUTIES OF OFFICERS

The duties of officers in the following outline are keyed to pages in this book on which their work is discussed. The page numbers appear after each specific duty.

a. *President*

    (1) Presides at unit meetings (52-55)
    (2) Presides at planning committee meeting (34-44)
    (3) Assigns responsibility (34-44)
    (4) Directs training (33, 34)
    (5) Represents unit on church Brotherhood council (18)
    (6) Presents needs of unit to Brotherhood director (18, 43, 44, 45, 118)
    (7) Communicates information on denominational programs (96-98)
    (8) Works to provide basic leadership publications and curriculum materials for unit members (43-45)
    (9) Receives and distributes funds (44, 45)

b. *Vice-president*

    (1) Builds attendance (109-115)
    (2) Increases enrollment (109-111)
    (3) Publicizes meetings (112-115)
    (4) Maintains fellowship (111, 112)
    (5) Participates in planning committee meeting (34-44)
    (6) Presides in absence of president (52-55)

c. *Secretary*

 (1) Keeps accurate records (115-120)
 (2) Shares records and minutes (117-119)
 (3) Serves in unit meetings (54)
 (4) Compiles and makes reports (117-120)
 (5) Prepares and maintains accurate mailing list (109, 114, 116)
 (6) Receives and distributes funds (44-45)
 (7) Participates in planning committee meeting (34-44)
 (8) Orders magazines: *Baptist Men's Journal, Guide,* and *Brotherhood Builder* (43)

d. *Mission Study Leader*

 (1) Helps plan unit meeting agenda (52-55)
 (2) Leads in presenting the mission study at unit meetings (54)
 (3) Provides other opportunities for men to study about missions (56-66)
 (4) Reports participation of men in mission study to secretary (118)
 (5) Participates in planning committee meetings (34-44)
 (6) Works with the secretary in securing needed curriculum materials (43, 57)
 (7) Organize for mission study requiring services of Mission Study Group Leader (23, 24, 60)
 (8) Encourage individual mission study (61)

e. *Mission Activity Leader*

 (1) Assists in conducting survey of church mission action needs (69-73)
 (2) Organizes for ongoing mission action and forms mission action and mission support groups (23, 73-81)

       (a) Considers the interest and abilities of men
       (b) Enlists individuals
       (c) Selects mission action group leaders, mission support group leaders and project leaders
   (3) Coordinates ongoing mission action (73-77)
   (4) Plans and coordinates mission action projects (23-24, 77-79)
   (5) Reports participation of men in activities to secretary (119)
   (6) Reports on mission action at unit meeting (55)
   (7) Leads men to support missions through prayer activities (85-91)
   (8) Leads men to support missions through giving activities (91-96)
   (9) Directs special projects as assigned by the church (98-105)
 (10) Participates in planning committee meetings (34-44)

f. *Mission Action Group Leader*
   (1) Leads the activities of mission action group under the supervision of the Mission Activity Leader (76-77)
       (a) Launch actions
          • Personal preparation
          • Orientation actions
          • Survey actions.
       (b) Continuing actions
          • Planning actions
          • Ministering and witnessing actions
          • Sharing and evaluating actions
          • In-service training actions.

    (2) Reports participation of men to Mission Activity Leader (119)

    (3) Makes request to Mission Activity Leader for persons to assist with mission action projects (77)

    (4) Makes request for finances to the Mission Activity Leader (76)

g. *Mission Study Group Leader*

    (1) Leads the activities of study group under the supervision of the Mission Study Leader (60-66)

    (2) Leads group in selecting a course of study (60)

    (3) Secures person to lead mission study (60)

    (4) Reports participation of individual men to Mission Study Leader (118)

    (5) Makes request for finances to the Mission Study Leader (118)

h. *Mission Support Group Leader*

    (1) Leads the activities of mission support group under the supervision of the Mission Activity Leader (90-96)

    (2) Confers with the Mission Activity Leader on activities proposed by the group (90-96)

    (3) Reports participation of men to the Mission Activity Leader (119)

    (4) Makes request for finances to the Mission Activity Leader (119)

i. *Project Leader*

    (1) Leads the activities of project group (77)

    (2) Confers with Mission Activity Leader on progress of project being conducted (77, 78)

(3) Reports participation of individual men to Mission Activity Leader (119)

(4) Makes request for finances to Mission Activity Leader (76)

F. STEPS FOR BEGINNING

Normally the Brotherhood director is responsible for beginning Baptist Men's units. In churches having no director, the pastor, minister of education, or another person may lead a committee appointed for this purpose. The group may be the nominating committee of the church.

Assuming the congregation favors the addition of Baptist Men's work to the church's existing programs, here are the steps to follow in establishing the organization and getting units started well:

1. DETERMINE ORGANIZATION

Review the section on organization on page 19-21 and compare the suggestions for grouping men with the needs of the church to determine the number of units to be organized.

2. CHOOSE OFFICERS

Select officers for each unit and present their names to the church for election.

3. TRAIN OFFICERS

Teach *Baptist Men in Missions* to the officers.

4. BEGIN PLANNING

Lead the officers to plan the work for the first year, following the planning procedure presented in Chapter II. The product should be plans in detail for the first unit meeting, plans in outline form for the next two unit meetings, themes for the next 12 months, and tentative plans for observing such special emphases as Baptist. Men's Day, home missions, foreign missions, and state missions.

The plans for the first unit meeting should include an interesting and informative agenda, ways to enlist men to attend, and arrangements for enrolling men in the unit.

5. PUBLICIZE MEETING

Announce the time, place and program of the first unit meeting using every available means for promotion.

6. CONDUCT UNIT MEETING

The first meeting should emphasize the part men will have in Baptist Men's work. Each unit may determine the approach it wants to take.

2. Guiding the Unit

CHAPTER OUTLINE

A. TRAINING
   1. OFFICERS
   2. MISSION ACTION GROUPS
   3. MISSION BOOK TEACHERS
   4. SPECIAL PROJECT LEADERS

B. PLANNING
   1. THE PLANNING COMMITTEE
   2. WHEN AND WHAT TO PLAN

C. FINANCING

D. EVALUATING

● Effective administration is essential to the success of a Baptist Men's unit. Good administration gives direction to the unit, inspires officers to perform their duties, creates enthusiasm in meetings and activities, heightens the interest of members, and assures the unit of continuing success.

Good administration rests with the president. However, each officer contributes to successful administration of a Baptist Men's unit work. This chapter deals with all areas of responsibility officers need to keep a unit moving toward its objective and goals, specifically training, planning, financing, and evaluating.

A. TRAINING

Effective administration is impossible without well trained officers.

Most associations provide training opportunities periodically for churches through the associational Brotherhood. The president needs to stay informed about these opportunities and make a special effort to involve men in them.

Men who need the training fall into four categories —unit officers, mission action groups, teachers of mission books, and leaders of special projects.

1. OFFICERS

The president is responsible for providing study opportunities for officers in the church. He should see that each officer completes a study of *Brotherhood Program of a Baptist Church,* a book on the concept and administration of Brotherhood work, and *Baptist Men in Missions,* a methods book on Baptist Men's work. He may provide for group study or see that men study the books individually.

The president can make arrangements through the Brotherhood council for men to study these Brotherhood concept and method books during Training Union when potential leaders can participate. In this way the church can provide a continuous supply of trained leaders to replace officers in existing units and to organize new units.

2. Mission Action Groups

The Mission Activity Leader and the president should make certain mission action groups have opportunity to train. Content and procedures for in-service training are contained in mission action group guides available from Baptist book stores. The in-service training action is a continuing activity of mission action groups.

3. Mission Book Teachers

Men who teach home and foreign mission graded series books should train in special classes before the mission study. This training may occur in the church or in a teacher training institute conducted by the association.

4. Special Project Leaders

Leaders of special projects of the church also need training. The content of the instructions will vary with each project. Suggested procedures for some special projects are on pages 78, 79.

B. PLANNING

Planning is deciding what to do and how to go about it. Planning helps an organization become a structure when people work together effectively. Worthwhile things very seldom just happen. They are planned with hours of work spent preparing for the happening.

Good planning requires a planning committee, regular planning times, and an agenda based on a unit's objective and goals.

1. THE PLANNING COMMITTEE

The planning committee of Baptist Men is comprised of the president, vice-president, secretary, Mission Study Leader, and Mission Activity Leader. The pastor, minister of education and Brotherhood director are ex-officio members of the committee. Other men may be invited to attend planning meetings when appropriate (such as a leader of a mission action group or a project leader).

The planning committee plans in detail how the work of the unit is to be accomplished. It is within this group that the officers present, coordinate, and evaluate their plans.

The planning committee should meet at least once a month. A definite time and place should be set for this meeting.

An effective planning committee is characterized by a good team spirit among the members and an ability and desire to plan efficiently.

a. *Team Spirit*

A team spirit among the members of the planning committee is essential to effective planning. Leaders wanting to develop team spirit should plan with purpose and develop fellowship among the men.

(1) Plan with Purpose

Committee members need to understand why planning with a purpose is necessary. Here are some reasons:
- Puts purpose into every study and activity
- Keeps individuals and group needs in focus
- Avoids duplicating and overlapping of work
- Helps select the best way for a group to work together to reach its goal

- Uses educational and administrative principles and methods
- Helps a unit know what it has accomplished and what remains to be done.

(2) Develop Fellowship

Many planning committees have learned to make planning meetings a meaningful fellowship. Fellowship may be developed through:

(a) A Meal

Some planning committees meet in the home of a committee member. By rotating, each member entertains the committee about twice a year. Planning after the meal is done in a relaxed atmosphere.

(b) Group Participation

Fellowship grows when all officers participate in the planning. The president should see that each officer understands what part he has in the planning.

(c) Recognition

The president should recognize the committee members by asking them to help with the report to the Baptist Men's unit. Each officer may be asked to present one of the recommendations or reports. For example, if the committee is recommending a plan to increase membership, the vice-president may be asked to present the recommendation. The Mission Study Leader may present a recommendation to conduct a special mission study.

b. *Effective Planning*

A planning committee should frequently examine its work to determine whether it is planning efficiently or poorly.

Some qualities which contribute to efficiency are good presiding officers, a meeting place with good planning environment, adequate planning tools, and a definite agenda for the planning meeting.

(1) The Presiding Officer

"What kind of person makes a good committee chairman? Think back over some of the committee meetings you have attended. How many of these chairmen have you known?

"The Boss. The Boss keeps his committee in line. He slaps down (verbally, of course) anyone who talks too much and continually nudges the shy members who don't talk as much as he thinks they should. He runs his committee with an iron fist and expects discipline. His voice is authoritative and brooks no argument. When he passes out assignments to members of the committee, he expects the jobs to be done right and on time. He's very much aware of the importance of his job—and of himself.

"The Man of Action. Results are all that count with the Man of Action. They may not be the right results, but that doesn't matter so long as something gets done. If the committee seems to be slowing down in its work, he quickly moves it on to the next topic, either promising to return to the other one later or assigning it to a subcommittee. To make absolutely sure that the committee winds up its meeting with plenty of decisions made, he comes prepared with his set of decisions. Using a variety of methods, he forces his decisions on the rest of the committee.

"The Agenda Addict. Closely related to the man of action, the Agenda Addict carefully leads his committee down an all-important list of things to be done and refuses to let it stray off course. He, too, wants results quickly and will be apt

to come to the meeting with some built-in results to force on the committee. Because of his carefully prepared agenda, he is unlikely to see how related topics have a bearing on his narrowly outlined topic. As a result his committee is apt to arrive at narrow, shallow decisions.

"The Watcher. Very different from the other three, the Watcher is content to let his committee members talk and work freely with no leadership. He figures if he just sits back and lets things take their own course, they'll work themselves out. He may be the one to call the meeting and outline the topic of discussion, but that's about as far as he'll go. The rest, he assumes, is up to the committee.

"Anyone familiar? You've probably known them all. This next type of leader is rarer than all, but if you've worked with him you probably felt that his was one of the best committee meetings you had had.

"The Democratic Leader. This fellow knows his job is important and he's confident that he, working with his committee members, can handle it. But he knows he must work with his group, not do their work for them. He knows he must have the skills to do these things:

- Help the committee members organize themselves into a group, not a collection of individuals.
- Determine what resources lie hidden within each person and how to release those resources.
- Help the group decide its own rules for the meetings.
- Encourage the group to be objectively critical of itself so that its work will be of high caliber.
- Help the members of the group create an atmosphere of freedom in the meetings so that everyone feels able to talk openly and honestly.
- Help the group develop methods of continually evaluating its own work.

"In short, The Democratic Leader encourages his committee to look at itself as a committee and to continually improve itself. This kind of leadership is not the easiest kind to use. It's much easier to tell a committee what you want and let them rubber stamp your plans. But the democratic process, developed and used skillfully, can inspire a group to far greater heights than the group might imagine." [1]

(2) The Meeting Place

Where should a planning committee meet? Should it meet in homes of the members, in a room at the church, or in a restaurant dining room? Either of these places may be acceptable if a good planning environment can be achieved. The following things should be considered before a meeting place is selected.

- Is it quiet?
- Will it be free of distractions?
- Is it well ventilated?
- Is it well lighted?
- Is there a table large enough for the men to sit around?
- Are there enough comfortable chairs?

The importance of these elements is often overlooked because the people in the meeting may be unaware of them. A poorly lighted room may not bother anyone at first, but if this difficulty causes a member to develop a headache, the efficiency of the committee will diminish. Poor ventilation may go unnoticed for awhile, but eventually drowsiness will begin to creep over the group and slow the work. Physical surroundings may not make a meeting successful, but they can contribute to its failure.

---

[1] Parker, Jack T. *The Collier Quick and Easy Guide to Running a Meeting,* New York: Collier Books, 1963, pp. 49-50.

(3) The Tools

Appropriate tools contribute to the success of any work. This is true of a planning committee. Some tools which the committee members need are:

- *Baptist Men's Journal*
- *Guide*
- *Brotherhood Builder*
- *Baptist Men's Record and Report* (secretary only)
- Calendars (church, association, state, SBC)
- List of mission needs.

The *Baptist Men's Journal* contains study materials for use during the mission study period of the unit meeting. All members of the Baptist Men's unit should receive this quarterly magazine.

Guide contains a suggested agenda for each monthly unit meeting during a quarter with appropriate ideas for each part of the agenda. Detailed helps for observing special events such as study of mission graded series books, mission offerings, and Baptist Men's Day are also in *Guide. Guide,* prepared especially for officers, contains suggestions in each issue for servicing the Baptist Men's unit.

The secretary's records and reports contain the information needed to plan and evaluate a unit's work.

The calendars (church, association, state, and SBC) help units plan and present activities when resources are available and in harmony with activities of other groups.

A list of mission action needs keeps before the committee the need for planning ways to involve men in ministering and witnessing to persons of special need or circumstance.

(4) The Meeting Agenda

Before the meeting the president should plan a tentative agenda. It should include:

- Scripture and prayer

- Reading of the minutes of the last meeting
- Reports of activities in progress (Mission Study Leader, Mission Activity Leader, vice-president and others)
- Evaluation of reports
- Planning for future
- Planning for the unit meetings
- Reports and request from the Brotherhood council
- Miscellaneous business.

Immediately after the opening prayer the president should discuss the tentative agenda with the committee, listing definite items to be discussed in the order of priority. The immediacy of an event and the amount of planning and promotion it will require usually determines priority.

Planning for the next unit meeting should not be allowed to take all of the planning time. The officers can eliminate this problem by bringing to the meeting well-thought-out written recommendations. Here are some suggestions for each officer.

The vice-president should be ready to present plans for promoting attendance. The secretary should provide a list of items left over from the last planning meeting and recommendations from the Brotherhood council and the Baptist Men's unit. Plans for presenting the mission study should be presented by the Mission Study Leader. Reports on the work of mission action groups and recommendations for future action should be presented by the Mission Activity Leader.

If these officers wait until they come to the meeting to begin doing their work, they will consume all of the time planning the unit meeting.

2. WHEN AND WHAT TO PLAN

Even though the planning committee meets monthly, planning should not be on a month-to-month basis. Ideally, the committee should look ahead as far as two years in their planning. It is true that officers are usually elected for one year. Nevertheless, they must accept the responsibility for leading the unit toward continual growth in quality and quantity.

A Baptist Men's unit which has been meeting regularly with less than a majority of men in the church attending and without a noticeable increase in interest or sense of direction is usually a unit with inadequate planning.

Needs vary from church to church. Therefore, mission education for men must be planned to suit the needs of the individual church.

Good planning is done on an annual, quarterly, and monthly basis. Here are some suggestions for each of these periods:

a. *Annually* (Before September)

Annual planning may occur during a monthly planning meeting. However, a special planning meeting will usually produce better results. If annual planning is done during a monthly planning meeting, more than the usual amount of time should be used. Here are some things to do:

- Review previously adopted long range goals.
- Revise goals if needed.
- Set new goals as needed for at least one year beyond the time for which goals have previously been adopted.
- Set dates of planning committee meeting and place in church calendar.
- Begin necessary plans to implement assignments from the Brotherhood council.
- Set dates of unit meetings for one year and place on church calendar.

- Adopt theme for each unit meeting during the year.
- Determine the type of meetings (dinner, cook-out, ladies' night, father-and-son retreat, etc.).
- Decide on speakers for special emphasis (public officials, missionaries, etc.).
- Set dates for special emphasis (foreign missions, home missions, Baptist Men's Day, state missions).
- Review current mission action survey and select new mission action opportunity.
- Set dates for membership drive.
- Set dates for leader training courses.
- List dates of state and associational Brotherhood meetings and tentatively plan representation.
- List projects of the church for which the unit may volunteer assistance and plan to support them.
- Estimate financial needs for one year (honorariums for speakers, extra meals, magazines, books, supplies, postage, etc.) and prepare budget requests for Brotherhood council to consider.
- Order supply of *Baptist Men's Journal* for all men, *Guide* for all officers, *Brotherhood Builder* for the president, and supplies for the year.

b. *Quarterly*

Quarterly planning is done during the last monthly planning meeting of each quarter. Here is a suggested agenda:

- Review annual plans to determine progress.
- Check progress of detailed plans for unit meetings in the next three months.
- See that all materials (printed, visual) needed for the next three meetings will be available.
- Make final assignments to officers for unit meetings for the next three months.

- Make final detailed plans (personnel, promotion, materials) for special emphasis occurring in the next three months. Detailed suggestions for planning special studies of books in the foreign and home mission graded series and observing Baptist Men's Day are in *Brotherhood Builder* which the president receives as a member of the Brotherhood council.
- Compare the number of *Baptist Men's Journals* being received with present enrollment and adjust as needed.
- Discuss new assignments from the Brotherhood council.

c. *Monthly*

Here is a suggested agenda for this planning meeting:
- Review annual and quarterly plans to determine progress.
- Discuss recommendations from the officers on plans for the next unit meeting. (See suggestions in *Guide*.)
- Check on attendance promotion plans.
- Arrange payment of all bills (meals, speaker, honorarium).
- Review reports of mission action groups and plan mission action report to the unit.
- Review reports of special projects.
- Discuss and write all recommendations to be made to the unit.

C. FINANCING

A Baptist Men's unit receives its financial support from the church. At the beginning of each year the planning committee should estimate the unit's needs for the year, considering such items as magazines, mission books, supplies, program expenses, and extra meals. This itemized list of needs should go to the Brotherhood council for inclusion in the Brotherhood's budget request to the church.

The Baptist Men's unit through its president may ask the Brotherhood council for authority to spend money when funds are needed. If the church does not have a Brotherhood council, the president should make the request to the appropriate person or body designated by the church.

The secretary will need to keep accurate records of all expenditures and include them in the unit's monthly report to the Brotherhood council or to the church if there is no council.

A Baptist Men's unit should not make a practice of collecting money from its members. A better method is to support the church's stewardship program and permit the church to support the unit financially.

D. EVALUATING

A unit's work should be evaluated to isolate strengths and weaknesses for the president to report to the Brotherhood council.

The following list of questions will help with the evaluation:

- Have the necessary officers been elected?
- Have officers studied *Baptist Men in Missions?*
- Did officers attend the last associational Brotherhood workshop?
- Did every officer receive a copy of *Guide* each quarter?
- Did each officer report to the planning committee on work done?

- Were all members and prospects in the church invited to attend meetings?
- Did secretary record attendance of men at unit meetings?
- Are suggestions in the *Baptist Men's Journal* and *Guide* used as a basis for the monthly mission study and activity period?
- Do members of the unit receive regular issues of the *Baptist Men's Journal?*
- Was opportunity provided for men to participate in foreign and home mission study?
- Were men encouraged to read mission books?
- Are Baptist Men engaged in any mission action within the community?
- Were men encouraged to participate in church offerings for home and foreign missions?
- Were men regularly encouraged to witness in mission situations in the community?
- Were men used in a special way in church projects (revivals, stewardship promotion, etc.)?

3. Teaching Missions

CHAPTER OUTLINE

A. CONTENT OF MISSION STUDY

　　1. BIBLICAL BASIS FOR CHRISTIAN MISSIONS
　　2. PROGRESS OF CHRISTIAN MISSIONS
　　3. CONTEMPORARY MISSIONS

B. MISSION STUDY OPPORTUNITIES

　　1. UNIT MEETINGS
　　2. SPECIAL GROUP STUDY
　　3. INDIVIDUAL STUDY

C. MISSION STUDY METHODS

　　1. PRESENTATION
　　2. DISCUSSION
　　3. RESEARCH AND EXPERIMENTATION
　　4. SPECIFIC LEARNING METHODS

• A Baptist Men's unit has a mandate from the church to inform men about the church's mission. This function of a Baptist Men's unit grows out of the mission teaching task churches have assigned to Brotherhood units. The content and methods used by a Baptist Men's unit to teach missions to men make up this chapter.

A. CONTENT OF MISSION STUDY

There are three major areas in the content of mission study. These are the biblical basis of missions, progress of Christian missions, and contemporary missions. The curriculum of Baptist Men is planned to provide learning experiences in all three areas. A brief discussion of this basic content of mission study follows:

1. BIBLICAL BASIS FOR CHRISTIAN MISSIONS

Major concepts in this area include the origin of missions, the predicament of all men, the covenant people, the life and teachings of Jesus, the promised redeemer, the redeemer revealed, the eternal purpose of God, and the nature and mission of the church.

Christian missions originated in the heart of God. "God is love" (1 John 4:8). It is this attribute of God's nature that gave birth to missions and make it possible for man to become a part of the divine plan for redeeming mankind. The words of John 3:16, "For God so loved the world that he gave his only begotten son," indicates the infinite character of God's concern for people who are lost through their disobedience and the limitlessness of his provision for their salvation.

To his disciples Jesus said, "Come ye after me, and I will make you to become fishers of men" (Mark 1:17). Through the method of example and teaching, Jesus led these men to understand God's plan.

Based on the affirmation that "Thou are the Christ the son of the living God" (Matthew 16:16), Jesus founded his church. He gave its members the mission of proclaiming the gospel to all people, everywhere. He said, "Go ye therefore, and teach all nations, baptizing them in the name of the Father and of the Son, and of the Holy Ghost: teaching them to observe all things whatsoever I have commanded you: and lo, I am with you always, even unto the end of the world" (Matthew 28:19-20).

The disciples interpreted this commission to mean placing all other affairs of life, even life itself, second to their mission of taking the gospel to all people. They went everywhere proclaiming the good news of God's redemptive love as expressed through Jesus Christ.

2. Progress of Christian Missions

Two broad categories characterize the progress of Christian missions. They are the beginning of missionary history and the development of missionary history.

The beginning of missionary history encompasses Pentecost, the scattering of the early Christians, the first missionaries, missionary expansion to the end of New Testament times, and missionary letters.

Within the development of missionary history are such areas of interest as early church missions (A.D. 100-313), early European missions (A.D. 313-800), Middle Ages (A.D. 800-1517), Reformation (A.D. 1517-1650), early missionary societies (A.D. 1650-1792), and modern missions (1792-   ).

The history of Christian missions begins in the New Testament. The Acts of the Apostles is an account of the development of the church's concept of its mission. The maturing church, which was first composed of Christian

Jews, became a dynamic force proclaiming that the gospel was for all people. Wherever Christians went, churches sprang up. These churches developed believers who proclaimed the gospel throughout the Roman Empire. From the first century until the present, the activities of the early church and the instruction Paul wrote in his letters have served as a pattern for missionary activities.

Generally, the progress of Christian missions includes the early success of Christianity, the decline in quality of Christianity after the advent of the "Holy Roman Empire," the struggle for survival during the Dark Ages, the rebirth of power through the Reformation, the beginning of the modern missionary movement at the close of the Eighteenth Century, and the activities of missionary societies and boards until the present.

The progress of Christian missions moved through the lives of Christians who held to firm convictions that they were on a mission for God. It is from the lives of these concerned Christians that the curriculum for Baptist Men's mission study draws some of its most stirring material.

3. Contemporary Missions

Current mission study must be set against a background of forces which affect world conditions. They include economic forces, technological forces, spiritual forces, socio-cultural forces, and political forces. Certain specific issues of rapid social change which affect missions are to be included such as family life, education, industrialization, nationalism, governmental influence, and civil rights.

In the area of general missions, men have an opportunity to study the philosophy of Christian missions, apologetics, and methods and techniques. The philosophy and strategy of other world religions and cults also are included in the curriculum. This study provides additional understanding of the challenge faced by contemporary Christian missions.

A study of missions would be incomplete without a look at the work of other Christian groups. These groups include other Baptists, other evangelical groups, Roman and Orthodox Catholics, and Christian sects.

The most significant area of contemporary missions for our study is the work of Southern Baptists. Included is current Southern Baptist mission work in the community, association, state, nation, and foreign countries, types of Southern Baptist mission work, and how Southern Baptists support mission work.

B. MISSION STUDY OPPORTUNITIES

Mission learning opportunities are provided by a Baptist Men's unit through unit meetings, special group studies, and individual studies.

1. UNIT MEETINGS

Most Baptist Men's units meet at a specific date and time. This meeting occurs at regular intervals, possibly weekly, bi-weekly or monthly.

The five most prevalent questions about a unit meeting are when should Baptist Men meet? How often? How long? What should be done at the meeting? What makes a meeting interesting?

a. *When Should Baptist Men Meet?*

There is no single time suggested for all units. Each unit must decide for itself, based upon the needs of the men and the church. When the men have chosen the time for the meeting, it should be approved by the church. It then becomes a regular part of the church calendar.

b. *How Often Should Baptist Men Meet?*

The Baptist Men's meeting should be held regularly at least once each month. Some units may meet more often. The best work is being carried on by units which meet monthly for the entire year.

Serious harm occurs when a Baptist Men's unit disbands or drifts during the summer months. A unit may vary the type of meetings. For example, summer is a time for outdoor meetings and activities.

c. *How Long Should the Meetings Last?*

The regular meeting should last about 60 minutes. Additional activities, such as a meal will require extra time.

d. *What Should Be Done at the Meeting?*

The unit meeting of Baptist Men is designed to involve men in mission learning experiences, motivate them to action, and provide an outlet to this motivation. It should be planned in detail by the planning committee.

A meeting agenda has five major elements. They are opening period, special feature period, mission study period, mission activity period, and closing period.

Suggestions for each element of the agenda are in *Guide,* a quarterly publication for officers of Baptist men.

The president should preside but may assign various phases of the agenda to others.

The following agenda is suggested. It may be rearranged if the change increases its value for a particular Baptist Men's unit.

(1) Opening Period

This period includes music, Scripture, prayer, and introduction and welcome of guests. The secretary checks attendance at this time.

(2) Special Feature Period

This time is devoted to ways to support missions through praying and giving. Such matters as church budgets, Cooperative Program, special offerings, and objects of prayer are emphasized. Suggested emphases for each month are in *Guide*.

(3) Mission Study Period

This is the period to present information about missions from material found in *Baptist Men's Journal,* using the procedures suggested in *Guide*. Planners will want to consider all of the suggestions in *Guide* based on the needs of the unit and adapt the most meaningful ones to the needs of the men. The Mission Study Leader should attempt to inject his own personality and imagination into the presentation as he seeks to increase the understanding of men about missions and to motivate them to become involved in missions.

Guide offers suggestions in three areas for the Mission Study Leader.

(a) Planning

Guide suggests materials that can be ordered, assignments to make, and other items necessary to properly prepare for the meeting.

(b) Presentation

Guide includes suggestions on how to develop the program. Some materials not found in the *Baptist Men's Journal* are placed in *Guide* to give the Mission Study Leader fresh approaches to challenge men.

(c) Alternate Approach

Guide includes alternate suggestions on how to present the information on missions in an interesting, informative manner.

(4) Mission Activity Period

During this period possible activities growing out of the information presentation are discussed and selected by the men using the voting process. The necessary groups for carrying out new mission activities are formed and notified of their assignments. This period also is used to discuss and approve recommendations from the planning committee.

(5) Closing Period

During this period, leaders express appreciation for work and lead in discussions of miscellaneous business. The meeting should close with prayer.

e. *What Makes a Meeting Interesting?*

Here are some helpful hints the planning committee may use to make the unit meeting come alive.
- Plan each part of the agenda in detail.
- Create an air of expectancy through effective publicity before the meeting.
- Create a relaxed and friendly atmosphere.
- Keep the agenda moving from one item to another without unnecessary comments.
- Use attractive posters and other visuals to present items on the agenda.
- Involve as many men as possible.
- Keep mission needs before the men.
- Begin on time and close on time.

2. SPECIAL GROUP STUDY

From time to time a Baptist Men's unit may sponsor special group studies. They may be for men only or the unit may join with the Woman's Missionary Union in sponsoring a mission study for men and women or for all age levels at the request of the church. Content may include books in the foreign and home mission graded series, mission books in the Seminary Extension Department, and general mission books in the Church Study Course.

Books on foreign missions and home missions provide men with the opportunity to consider in depth particular phases of Southern Baptist mission work. The books are prepared annually by the Foreign Mission Board and Home Mission Board in consultation with the Brotherhood Commission and Woman's Missionary Union. These books are frequently taught during world mission conferences (schools of missions).

A special group study of missions, involving men may be church-wide for all age levels, for men and women, or for men only and held in the church, in a retreat setting, or at another site in a seminar form. Here are some of the more popular methods used in mission study.

a. *Church-Wide Mission Study*

Best materials available for a church-wide mission study are the Foreign Mission Graded Series and Home Mission Graded Series which provide books for adults, youth, and children.

For a church-wide mission study for all age levels the pastor may ask the Brotherhood and WMU councils to plan and coordinate the activities. Or a Baptist Men's unit may be asked to take the lead. In this event here is a suggested procedure:

- Set date and place it on the church calendar.
- Enlist teachers for each age group.
- Order mission study books and teaching aids from the Baptist book store and free materials from the Foreign Mission Board and Home Mission Board.
- Assign rooms.
- Secure equipment such as chalkboards, projectors, screens, and easels. (The teachers should be consulted to determine what equipment they need.)
- Make plans to promote attendance.

Planners will want to make it clear the church mission study is for everyone, not just for the members of the mission organizations.

b. *Mission Study for Men and Women*

The same basic preparation suggested for a church-wide mission study should be made for the adult mission study. The president and the Mission Study Leader of Baptist Men and the president and the Study Chairman of Baptist Women may serve as the steering committee.

c. *Mission Study for Men*

For this study the Mission Study Leader will develop plans and present them to the Baptist Men's planning committee for discussion and approval. Types of studies for men to consider are:

(1) Book Review

A review of the mission study book in one or two nights may be desirable. However, the men should have at least three hours to review the book.

One person may be selected to present the review, or different members of Baptist Men may present a chapter each. (Allow each man 20-30 minutes to review his chapter.)

(2) Family Study

Men may lead their families in a discussion of mission books. Each child may contribute to the discussion by relating things he has learned from reading the book prepared for his age group. The family study plan should be used if the church does not provide mission study opportunities for all age groups.

(3) Mission Study Seminar

There are at least two approaches to consider when preparing to conduct a seminar. One is advance enrollment of men for a specific time and place. In using this approach, it is wise to distribute a copy of study materials to each man as he enrolls. Instructions should include a request to read the material and acquaint himself with the content to be discussed before coming to the seminar.

Another approach is simply to distribute the mission materials after the men arrive. In this case the mission material is distributed and time is alloted for it to be read. The group may discuss all of the questions as a whole or break up into smaller groups to discuss assigned questions. If the last method is used, the entire group should reassemble and appraise the conclusions of each of the smaller groups.

At the appointed time for the seminar, a discussion leader calls the meeting to order. After an opening prayer he introduces any resource persons who have been enlisted, names a recorder to take notes, and carefully explains the procedure the men will follow. Here is a suggested procedure.

(a) The Background Statement

The discussion leader reads the background statement, which will introduce the subject for discussion.

(b) Group Division and Question Assignment

Following the reading of the background statement, the discussion leader directs the seminar to form groups and appoint chairmen. Then the discussion leader assigns each group a question. After the groups are organized, the discussion leader, recorder, and resource persons visit different groups and contribute to the discussion.

(c) The Call to Order

The discussion leader calls the seminar to order after a maximum of 30 minutes of group discussion, asking for reports from the group chairmen.

After each report the resource person and other members of the seminar may want to comment on the answers given by the group spokesman. A maximum of five minutes should be devoted to the answer and comments on the question discussed by each group.

If time remains after group reports are heard, the discussion leader may open the meeting to general discussion of the subject under consideration. The discussion leader tries to reach conclusions for a summary statement for the entire seminar.

(d) The Summary

Five minutes before the end of the period the discussion leader cuts off discussion and calls on the recorder to give the closing summary. This summary should contain the conclusions reached by the entire group on each of the questions.

(e) Adjourn

The discussion leader adjourns the meeting at the time agreed on beforehand. Any delay may reduce enthusiasm for future seminars.

(f) Reporting

Following adjournment, the discussion leader, resource persons, and the recorder write out the summary statement adopted by the seminar. The discussion leader and recorder edit the statement, have it duplicated, and distribute it to each participant. A copy should go into the records of the Baptist Men's unit.

(4) Mission Study Retreat

A mission study retreat may or may not be different from other special group studies. However, it does need special planning to be successful.

Some Baptist men have received a new appreciation for missions during a study at a week-end retreat at a lodge or camp. The mission study retreat could begin on Friday evening and close Saturday afternoon.

Arrangements for sleeping quarters, meals, transportation, and teaching aids should be made well in advance of the retreat. Plans should allow for periods of worship, discussion, and fellowship between mission study sessions.

(5) Mission Study Groups

Mission study groups may be formed by the Mission Study Leader to continue study of particular areas of missions in depth.

A leader responsible for arranging the meeting place and leading the activities should be designated for each group.

Activities may consist of study in particular geographical areas of missions, Bible study related to missions, mission books, or depth study of the church's mission in the community. The Mission Study Group Leader may lead the discussions, invite outside speakers, or ask one of the group members to lead the discussion.

3. INDIVIDUAL STUDY

Men who do not or cannot attend group mission study should be motivated to do individual study. One way to encourage individual study is to ask a man to read a book and give a brief report on it during the special feature period of the Baptist Men's unit meeting.

C. MISSION STUDY METHODS

Learning methods combine with mission content to help persons seek and find knowledge that changes attitudes, values, and behavior.

There are three basic types of learning methods. Frequently, two or more should be used together. They are presentation (when one or more persons speak to the group), discussion (when members discuss a subject within the group or with resource persons), and research and experimentation (when members study and test a subject and bring their findings to the group).

1. PRESENTATION

The presentation method should be used when the group needs factual information. A speaker, panel, interview, or film may be the center of the presentation. Other types of presentation methods may be used.

The presentation method is composed of three steps:

a. *Select and Introduce the Presentation with Care*

The purpose of an introduction is not to express appreciation for the speaker, book, or film, but to arouse the group's interest and to prepare them to "receive."

b. *Prepare the Group*

Before the presentation, efforts should be made to help

the group "receive." The leader may ask each person to think of a question to ask a speaker and assign teams to listen for a specific answer to a problem or question. Each person may be instructed to take notes on ideas to list under headings already presented to the group.

c. *Plan for a Response*

Response may be in the form of a question period or general group discussion. The leader may ask for reports from listening teams or for specific answers to questions.

2. DISCUSSION

The discussion method is composed of four steps:

a. *Choose Topics Suitable for Discussion*

The topic should be important to the group and one to which all can contribute. If the topic is not within the experience of the group, members may have an opportunity to prepare beforehand by listening thoughtfully to a presentation or through outside reading and study.

Constructive learning seldom comes from discussion of a subject about which group members have strong feelings. The result is usually a heated argument. Different points of view may be presented by using a panel or by asking each person to respond, placing a time limit on each response.

An introductory statement by the leader may tell the group that there are many opinions on the subject and that there is no one right answer. Therefore, the discussion should not aim for any one conclusion.

b. *Formulate Questions with Care*

The purpose of questions is to stimulate thought and produce interaction between persons. The leader should avoid "yes or no" questions since they call for a minimum of mind searching, and there is nothing more to say. Questions which direct discussion toward conclusions already made slant the discussion in one direction and defeat the approach. For example: "How will this discussion help our group?" This assumes that each person should find it helpful. A better question would be "Will this discussion help our group? If so, how?"

c. *Discussion Leader Must Prepare*

After a suitable topic has been chosen, this process may prove helpful in planning for the discussion:

- State topic clearly.
- Prepare an interesting way to begin.
- List aspects of the subject which need to be discussed.
- Plan to relate one or two personal experiences.
- Select a few brief illustrations.
- Plan several ways to conclude the discussion.

The conclusion might be in the form of a summary, a meaningful quotation, or a plan for evaluating.

d. *Discussion Leader Sets Example*

The discussion leader sets an example for others who are learning to be responsible discussion participants. He should be more eager to hear what others have to say than to present his own ideas on the subject.

The discussion leader should:

- Make sure that everyone hears and understands the question.
- Wait patiently for persons to speak.
- Listen and accept what each person has to say.
- Respect each individual and his views.
- Restate any idea which deserves more attention from the group.

- Repeat in his own words something that an inarticulate person attempts to say.
- Offer information if and when it is needed.

3. Research and Experimentation

Three statements should be kept in mind when making assignments. They are:

- Assign work only as it contributes purposefully to the groups' learning.
- Make each assignment, showing its purpose and introducing it in such a way that those who are to carry it out see its purpose and know what to look for.
- Plan interesting, purposeful ways to use the findings to aid the group in its learning.

Leaders making an assignment should not say: "Bring us a report," but should make the assignment more specific by saying; "Bring four or five ideas for solving this problem" or "Bring an outline of the writer's viewpoint."

4. Specific Learning Methods

Persons leading mission study should be familiar with the terms used to indicate specific methods which add variety and effectiveness to the three general types of learning methods. Here are the methods:

a. *Group Discussion* (5-20 persons)

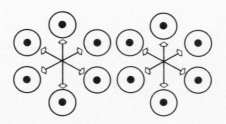

b. *Buzz Groups* (2-6 persons)

Group discusses for three to six minutes a question or topic or performs a task such as choosing a question to ask a speaker.

c. *Work Groups*

About six persons work together to complete an assignment and report to a larger group.

d. *Listening Teams*

A large group is divided into teams to obtain information about a topic or answers to a question. After the presentation, members comment or the group meets and chooses a spokesman.

e. *Panel* (3-6 persons)

Panel members talk together before the audience. The subject should be introduced by a moderator.

f. *Symposium*

Several persons present brief talks on different phases of a subject or offer different points of view and express different attitudes.

g. *Interview*

One member asks resource persons questions, directing the questions toward the interests and needs of the audience.

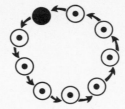

h. *Circular Response*

Each member in turn expresses his thinking on the subject under discussion, no one speaking until his time comes again.

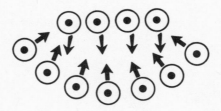

i. *Forum*

This is a group discussion which follows a speaker, panel, film, or resource person.

j. *Brainstorming*

Group members offer as many spontaneous ideas as possible about a subject. They are not evaluated until later.

k. *Field Trip*

This is a tour or visit where the group can learn through observation and study.

l. *Speech, Talk, or Lecture*

A speaker gives information, arouses interest in a new idea, or develops new meaning for what the group has been doing.

4. Engaging in Mission Action

CHAPTER OUTLINE

A. DISCOVERING NEEDS
1. IN-CHURCH SURVEY
2. COMMUNITY SURVEY

B. PLANNING FOR MISSION ACTION

C. CONDUCTING MISSION ACTION
1. THROUGH ON-GOING ACTION
2. THROUGH MISSION ACTION PROJECTS

D. BROTHERHOOD AND WMU JOINT MISSION ACTION GROUPS
1. WHEN ARE JOINT MISSION ACTION GROUPS FORMED?
2. HOW ARE JOINT MISSION ACTION GROUPS FORMED?
3. HOW IS THE WORK OF A JOINT MISSION ACTION GROUP COORDINATED AND REPORTED?

E. RESOURCES FOR MISSION ACTION
1. *Mission Action Survey Guide*
2. *Mission Action Projects Guide*
3. *Mission Action Group Guides*

● Through mission action a Baptist Men's unit becomes an arm of the church reaching out to people of special need or circumstance. In a real sense mission action is evangelism, education, stewardship, ministry, and missions at work in the name of Christ.

In every community there are persons not being reached by the church in its usual programs of outreach. Barriers, real and imagined, stand between these people and the church. They may be social, economic, emotional, physical, cultural, linguistic, or racial. Churches must teach Christians how to overcome barriers if these people are to be won to Christ. The special effort a church makes to extend its ministry and witness to people behind barriers of special needs and circumstances is known as mission action. The nature of this work as part of the church's mission program suggests the use of the Brotherhood organization, particularly Baptist Men's units.

This chapter does not tell men how to perform every mission action but provides a general outline of the concept, identifies methods for initiating and leading a program of mission action, and suggests specific resources for additional guidance. Key officer of Baptist Men in this endeavor is the Mission Activity Leader.

Successful mission action programs have common ingredients—discovering needs, planning, conducting the activities, and resources.

A. DISCOVERING NEEDS

Often a church is unaware of people who have special needs unless the members make a special effort to find them. The best approach is to take a mission action survey.

The *Mission Action Survey Guide* (available from Baptist book store) contains specific instructions on how to conduct a mission action survey. The Mission Activity Leader should become familiar with the contents of this book as he prepares to lead in the mission action survey as a representative of his Baptist Men's unit or his Brotherhood organization as a whole.

The purpose of the mission action survey is to find answers to the following questions:

- Where are the persons who have special need?
- What kind of needs do persons or groups have and what is the extent of their needs?
- What can our church do to meet or help meet these needs?

Answers to these questions may be secured by consulting with the following persons:

- Pastor and church staff
- Church members, particularly those who serve professionally as judges, welfare workers, school officials, and law enforcement officers
- Associational superintendent of missions
- Associational Brotherhood director and/or Woman's Missionary Union director
- Public school officials
- Government and private social agencies
- Courts (family, domestic, juvenile)
- Directors of institutions.

The mission action survey should be conducted by the officers of Brotherhood and Woman's Missionary Union or a special committee appointed by the church. All findings and plans should be coordinated with the church council before the church considers any recommendation to participate in a mission action.

There are two parts to a mission action survey: in-church and community.

The in-church survey is a means of gathering information from individual church members concerning needs of persons and moral issues of which they have personal knowledge.

The community survey is a survey of community agencies and institutions.

A survey is effective only when it has the support of the major part of the congregation. Therefore, it is important to inform the congregation of the significance of the survey.

Ways to help the congregation become informed are to print information concerning needs and issues in the church bulletin or church paper and present to the congregation speakers such as judges, welfare workers, school officials and members of the church who are aware of people in need.

1. In-Church Survey

A three-step procedure is suggested in conducting the in-church survey. It calls for (a) the use of survey forms (available from Baptist book store), (b) the determination of the extent of survey (how many people to be surveyed?) and (c) the selection of a method for conducting the survey.

Choices of methods include distributing forms to adults in church services or organizational meetings, organizing a telephone survey, or mailing forms to adult church members.

In following up on the survey, this process is recommended:

- Contact persons who gave incomplete information to get additional information such as name of person in need.
- Compile information (use compilation form in the *Mission Action Survey Guide*).
- Select needs to be met and assign contact persons.

2. COMMUNITY SURVEY

The community survey is a study of the area the church can reach with an effective ministry. Before conducting the community survey, a conference with the associational superintendent of missions, the associational Brotherhood director, and the associational WMU director may determine if work is already underway.

Here is a suggested procedure for conducting the survey:

- Compile a list of community agencies and institutions serving the community, including Community Service Council, Welfare Council, etc. Special forms are in the *Mission Action Survey Guide* for use in interviewing heads of these institutions and agencies. Work through the Volunteer Bureau if one exists in the community.
- Interview heads of agencies and institutions, using questions of this nature:
  —What kind of service does the agency or institution offer?
  —Does the institution need any volunteer assistance from individuals or groups?
  —If assistance is needed, what type? What skills are required? How much time is required?
  —What will be expected of your church if it renders a service?
  —Does the institution have rules about religious activities?

B. PLANNING FOR MISSION ACTION

To determine the needs to be met, the names of persons and institutions needing help should be listed in rank (1, 2, 3) according to the greatest need.

The next step is to present a proposal to the church council with a suggestion that the council review the plan in the light of resources available (people, finances, facilities, etc.) and establish priority on needs the church should begin to meet now.

The council should suggest that the church assign responsibility for the mission action to the Brotherhood and WMU.

The church council's recommendation to the church should contain the following information:

- List of needs in order of priority
- The actions which they recommend to the church
- Assignment of responsibility for each mission action proposed. (If work requires funds for employment of personnel or purchase of facilities, the missions committee may be asked to handle the administrative work.)

Once the Brotherhood and WMU assume responsibility for conducting the mission action, the Brotherhood council will make appropriate assignments for mission action responsibility to the Baptist Men's unit.

C. CONDUCTING MISSION ACTION

1. THROUGH ON-GOING ACTION

One of the best ways a Baptist Men's unit can meet needs is to form mission action groups to sustain an organized effort in behalf of the church. Meeting human need requires persons who are willing to learn how to minister and to witness in a specific category of work and persons who remain faithful over a long enough period of time to make a lasting contribution.

Adults and young people should volunteer for work in a mission action group according to their interest and aptitude for the kind of work to be done. The group will engage in a continuing cycle of action, usually lasting at least one year, working under the direction of a group leader. To support the primary actions of ministry and witness, group members engage in orientation actions, survey actions, planning actions, sharing and evaluation actions, and in-service training actions.

Groups usually meet at least once each month at a time convenient to group members. The emphasis is on mission action. Only the meetings necessary to prepare members for the work and to share experiences are conducted.

In the formation of mission action groups, the Brotherhood council has a major coordination role. After broad categories of need for mission action have been determined, the formation of groups could follow this pattern:

a. *Determine the Kinds of Mission Groups to Be Formed*

Initiative at this point is taken by the councils of Brotherhood and the Woman's Missionary Union working together. How should mission action groups be formed? Here are some possible groupings:

- A group of Baptist Men's unit members
- The entire membership of a small Baptist Men's unit
- A group of men and women (Baptist Men and Baptist Women working together).

In most churches groups will be easier to manage if they are formed along organizational lines—i.e., Baptist Men. It is possible, however, to cut across organizational lines.

b. *Inform Persons of Needs and Sign Up Volunteers*

Groups are formed by persons who volunteer on the basis of interest in and concern for the work being done.

When a unit discovers community needs and determines which needs it will attempt to meet, persons are asked to volunteer to serve in each area of work to be undertaken.

Church members must be informed of the opportunities for service through groups. Woman's Missionary Union and Brotherhood may want to work together in an interpretation campaign, or each may work separately.

Men who are not enrolled in a Baptist Men's unit shouldn't be overlooked. Some who will not be interested in other facets of the unit works will join a mission action group. Leaders will want to encourage these persons to participate to the limit of their interests, but not insist they participate in every phase of Baptist Men's work.

The Brotherhood council will coordinate the process of informing church members of opportunities.

Ideas about how to inform persons of the work to be undertaken are varied. No one way is best. Several ways can be used simultaneously. Here are some suggestions:

- Present the needs by the use of slides or by having someone tell of certain types of need in the community.
- Use an attractive announcement booklet to outline mission action opportunities.
- Plan a "look-see tour" to acquaint persons with the possibilities and give them an opportunity to sign up for work.
- Place in church bulletins announcements of mission action work to be started; request persons to indicate the work they would like to do.
- Invite the men of the church to a supper and interpret the work being undertaken. Allow them to sign up for service.

c. *Determine the Number of Groups to Be Formed and Enlist Leaders*

The sign-up process is like a preregistration. Signing up indicates the number of persons interested. From this response, the number of interested groups to be formed can be determined.

Groups can be small—three to six persons working together. Or there may be as many as 12 or 14 in the group. When an action group reaches 14 members, it is better to form another group.

The president and Mission Activity Leader enlist leaders for the groups attached to their units. Group leaders may be invited to attend meetings of the planning committee, especially when their work is being discussed.

d. *Train Leaders and Provide Resources for Group Work*

All Mission Action Group Leaders in Baptist Men may be trained together.

Broad plans for the training session should be made by the planning committee in consultation with the Brotherhood council.

The session should be based on the contents of the mission action group guides and how to use them. Each group member will need a group guide for the work being conducted.

Group leaders need to understand how to get money to buy additional materials and to conduct the work. If the Baptist Men's unit has planned wisely, its budget will include funds to conduct mission action. This is one reason for involving the church council and congregation in deciding what needs will be met. When the church is committed to getting the work done, it will provide the money to do it.

e. *Begin Group Action*

After all the groundwork has been laid, the groups begin their work. They engage in a cycle of actions based on guidance in the mission action group guides. Group progress is reported to the Baptist Men's unit regularly.

The Brotherhood council through the Brotherhood director reports progress in mission action to the congregation.

2. THROUGH MISSION ACTION PROJECTS

a. *Procedure*

As a rule mission action is conducted on the basis of need and for long periods of time. But when the need for a project (short-term activity) does emerge, Baptist Men stand ready to provide organization and leadership for conducting it. The process for planning, conducting, and evaluating mission action projects is in the *Mission Action Projects Guide.* This book also contains an exhaustive list of projects in more than 12 categories of need.

A leader should be chosen for each project and members of the unit asked to volunteer to serve on the project. The Mission Activity Leader may lead the project, especially if the unit has only one project at a time.

A project is short-term with a distinguishable beginning and ending.

When choosing a project, the following questions should be considered:

- Does project meet real need?
- Does it allow members to bear a positive Christian witness?
- Is the need being met by some other group?

- Does the organization have the resources (time, money, skills) to conduct the project?
- Will the project respect the dignity, pride, and personality of the persons being helped?
- Are members of the organization sufficiently interested to see the project through?

After each project, those participating should take time to evaluate their work by considering the following questions:

- Were the plans adequate?
- Were the members of the organization adequately prepared?
- Were the techniques suitable and well used?
- Did members encounter problems that they were unable to cope with adequately?
- Did members establish meaningful relationships with the persons helped?
- In what ways were these evidences of spiritual growth on the part of the helped and the helpers?

b. *Relationship*

Projects are related to the other work of the organization, therefore the need for projects may arise in three ways:

(1) Projects as Follow-Through to Study

For example, the unit studies about internationals. The interest created leads to conducting a single service to internationals such as an open house for internationals.

(2) Projects in Response to a Request from Mission Action Groups

For example, the mission action group working with economically disadvantaged persons decides to have a mission Vacation Bible School. They need assistance with transportation, teaching, crafts, and refreshments.

(3) Projects in Response to Other Needs

For example, an emergency is created by fire or some other tragedy. Assistance is needed for persons suffering loss.

D. BROTHERHOOD AND WMU JOINT MISSION ACTION GROUPS

A joint mission group is a mission action group in which the Woman's Missionary Union and the Brotherhood share responsibility for organizing, leading, and coordinating and in which both men and women participate.

1. WHEN ARE JOINT MISSION ACTION GROUPS FORMED?

Joint mission action groups are formed when services of both men and women are required to meet the needs of a particular target group. An example is in prisoner rehabilitation when mission action is performed with male and female prisoners. Meeting the needs of the prisoner's family usually requires the services of women as well as men.

A second occasion for joint mission action groups is when married couples working together can provide more effective services for a particular target group. An example is when sponsors or foster parents are needed in juvenile rehabilitation and in work with internationals.

A third time when joint mission action groups are needed is when the needs of the target group exceed the resources of either Woman's Missionary Union or Brotherhood. An example is when there is a need for a mission group to work with aging but only three men and two women want to participate in this group.

2. HOW ARE JOINT MISSION ACTION GROUPS FORMED?

When forming a joint mission action group, the Brotherhood director and the Woman's Missionary Union director should decide which organization will take the initiative for forming the group.

For example, the church council assigns to Brotherhood and Woman's Missionary Union the responsibility for work with internationals. The directors meet and decide that Baptist Men should lead in forming the joint mission action group.

Through the president of Baptist Men, the Mission Activity Leader is notified that he is to form the joint action group. After contacting the Baptist Women's president(s) to receive names of women who have expressed an interest in working with internationals, he proceeds to form the group by following the same procedure used by Baptist Men to form other mission action groups. For example, the Baptist Men's president, in conference with the Mission Activity Leader, appoints the group leader. In WMU the group leader is elected just as are all other Baptist Women or YWA officers.

The duties of the leader of a joint mission action group are the same as the duties of a leader of a mission action group made up of all men or all women.

The assistant group leader assists the group leader as needed and reports on the work of the group to his unit.

3. HOW IS THE WORK OF A JOINT MISSION ACTION GROUP COORDINATED AND REPORTED?

Responsibility for coordinating and reporting the work of a joint mission action group is assigned to the unit which has the initiative for forming the group. Normally, the Mission Activity Leader or chairman (Baptist Women) of that unit will perform the same responsibilities for a joint mission action group as he does for other mission action groups within his or her organization.

The group leader reports to the Mission Activity Leader or chairman (Baptist Women) of the sponsoring unit. The assistant group leader reports to the Mission Activity Leader or chairman (Baptist Women) of the other unit. Each organization's (WMU and Brotherhood) report to the church includes the number of its members participating in joint mission action groups.

E. RESOURCES FOR MISSION ACTION

1. *Mission Action Survey Guide*

This book provides a church help in discovering mission action needs, selecting needs to be met, and assigning responsibilities for meeting needs.

2. *Mission Action Projects Guide*

This book contains background information and project suggestions in more than 12 categories of need.

3. *Mission Action Group Guides*

These books guide mission action groups in on-going mission action. Guides available include:

- *Mission Action Group Guide: Economically Disadvantaged*
- *Mission Action Group Guide: Internationals*
- *Mission Action Group Guide: Juvenile Delinquents*
- *Mission Action Group Guide: Language Groups*
- *Mission Action Group Guide: The Sick*

- *Mission Action Group Guide: Combating Moral Problems*
- *Mission Action Group Guide: Nonreaders*
- *Mission Action Group Guide: Prisoner Rehabilitation*
- *Mission Action Group Guide: Aging*
- *Mission Action Group Guide: Negroes* *
- *Mission Action Group Guide: Headliners*
- *Mission Action Group Guide: Military*
- *Mission Action Group Guide: Resort Areas*

All of these resources are available in Baptist book stores.

Mission action group guides in other areas will be produced by the Brotherhood Commission and Woman's Missionary Union as these needs emerge.

---

* Published by the Brotherhood Commission in response to the Statement of Concern, adopted in the annual meeting of the Southern Baptist Convention, Houston, 1968.

5. *Enlarging Mission Support*

CHAPTER OUTLINE

A. THROUGH PRAYING AND GIVING

1. THROUGH PRAYING
2. THROUGH GIVING

B. PROVIDING AND INTERPRETING INFORMATION

1. SECURING INFORMATION
2. COMMUNICATING INFORMATION

C. CONDUCTING SPECIAL PROJECTS

1. SUPPORTING REVIVAL MEETINGS
2. STARTING A CHURCH TYPE MISSION
3. STEWARDSHIP CAMPAIGNS
4. OTHER MISSION ASSISTANCE

● A Baptist Men's unit provides a church three ways to enlarge its witness and ministry in the world. First, world mission support is enlarged through praying and giving by men who become concerned about mission needs.

Second, a Baptist Men's unit provides a channel for communicating to men information about the programs of the church and the denomination. In this way men become better informed about mission needs and ways they can become personally involved in meeting the needs.

Third, through church projects a Baptist Men's unit joins with other church program organizations to build a strong home base for world missions.

A. THROUGH PRAYING AND GIVING

Support world missions through praying and giving is the third task of Baptist Men. In fulfilling this task a Baptist Men's unit brings both spiritual and financial powers in focus on world needs. The object of praying and giving is to support mission work being conducted by churches through representative mission programs of the association, state and Southern Baptist Convention.

Prayer links a Baptist Men's unit with missions efforts around the world and acknowledges that divine resources are essential to effective missions work.

Giving allows Baptist men to support missions with their financial resources. It is one way each man can become personally involved in missions.

The purpose of this chapter is to suggest ways a Baptist Men's unit may accomplish this task. Praying and giving, with activities for each, are discussed separately. A Baptist Men's unit may vary the activities to suit its needs.

1. THROUGH PRAYING

The Baptist Men's unit leads men to pray for world missions through unit meetings, during special seasons of prayer, in prayer groups, and family and individual prayer.

a. *During Unit Meetings*

Prayer should occupy a significant place in every Baptist Men's unit meeting. The president may present objects of prayer during the opening period and ask several men to pray. He may ask each man to pray for one or more of the objects. Here are some areas to consider when making the list:

- Mission action needs in the community
- The work of mission action groups
- Special projects of the church such as revivals and stewardship emphasis
- The work of the association such as beginning church-type missions, institutional missions, simultaneous evangelistic efforts, training programs, and schools of missions
- Home and foreign missionaries whose names appear on the prayer calendar of *Home Life* and *Open Windows*
- Special areas of home mission work such as new work, special projects, and crisis areas listed in *Guide*
- Other mission needs known to individual men in the meeting.

The special feature period of the unit meeting also will provide time and specific objects for prayer.

b. *During Special Seasons of Prayer*

The observance of special seasons of prayer for state,

home, and foreign missions in many churches has become a church-wide emphasis. Baptist Men's units are taking an active part in planning and promoting these prayer seasons. Men usually participate in a mission prayer breakfast, prayer retreat, mid-week prayer service, Sunday School and Training Union assemblies, and congregational worship.

(1) Mission Prayer Breakfast

The mission prayer breakfast has become popular with Baptist men. It may be planned for any day in the week. Being at an early hour, men may attend before going to work. Slightly more time is available when a prayer breakfast is on Sunday.

The breakfast should be planned well. An atmosphere of reverence should prevail. The men should sense immediately that it is not a social occasion. Here are some helpful hints:

- Emphasize the real purpose of the meeting when promoting attendance and emphasize food service as a matter of convenience.
- Create an atmosphere of reverence. Appropriate music before and during the meal will help.
- Avoid announcements, welcoming speeches and other items not related to the purpose of the meeting.
- Present brief information on the major area of concern. For example, if the breakfast is during the week of prayer for foreign missions, a brief filmstrip on an area of foreign missions would be appropriate.
- List the objects of prayer and place a copy by each plate.
- Read the list of prayer objects and ask different men to pray for one object. Undue attention to a

time schedule may impair the spirit of the meeting. Nevertheless, the presiding officer should be aware of the time allowed. Usually a prayer breakfast should not last more than one hour. A presiding officer will find it helpful to have in mind a schedule similar to the one which follows:

6:30—Scripture Reading and Prayer
6:35—Breakfast
6:55—Informational Items
7:00—Objects of Prayer
7:10—Season of Prayer
7:30—Adjourn

(2) Mission Prayer Retreats

The mission prayer retreat provides time and opportunity for men to withdraw from distractions to seek the will of God through Scripture reading, mission study, and prayer.

A retreat is more effective if it is held in a quiet place free as possible from interferences such as telephones, television, or interruptions by persons not participating in the activity. An out-of-doors location away from the city or town may be the most appropriate choice. A retreat may be held in a chapel, church, home or on a college campus. State convention assembly grounds and camps also are usually excellent locations.

A prayer retreat may be for one day or longer. From Friday evening until Saturday afternoon may be the best period because more men are free from their jobs at this time.

One person should lead the retreat. He will ask others to assist in Bible study, mission study, prayer periods, and music. His role is to quietly guide the activities.

Plans should be made well in advance to allow time for men to arrange their schedules so they can attend. The time, date, and purpose of the retreat should be announced in all church meetings attended by men. The church bulletin and church paper are good vehicles to publicize the retreat.

The time schedule of the retreat should be flexible and unhurried. Nevertheless, to make the retreat meaningful, time must be divided to allow for balance in activities. Here is a suggested schedule for one day:

9:30—Group Singing and Prayer
9:40—Mission Study
10:40—Group Discussion
11:00—Season of Prayer
11:15—Individual Reading and Meditation
12:00—Lunch
1:00—Mission Study
2:30—Group Discussion
2:45—Season of Prayer
3:00—Adjourn

The mission study may be based on a mission study book with one person teaching a chapter each. The study will be more meaningful if the men have read the book before coming to the retreat.

Discussions may be with the entire group assembled or they may divide into smaller groups to discuss assigned topics.

(3) Mid-Week Prayer Service

The pastor may ask a Baptist Men's unit to take charge of the mid-week prayer services during the weeks of prayer for home and foreign missions. Or, he may suggest that the unit join with Baptist Women in conducting the prayer meeting. In either event the men should be ready to contribute to this occasion.

As in other mission events, plans should include worship in song and Scripture reading, information on missions, and opportunity for several persons to participate by praying for specific needs and missionaries.

The mission information may come from articles in *Baptist Men's Journal* or a mission study book. Only brief items should be presented, allowing ample time for prayer.

(4) Sunday School and Training Union Assemblies

On the Sundays which begin the weeks of prayer for home and foreign missions, many Sunday School and Training Union assembly programs are on missions. A Baptist Men's unit may volunteer to assign a man to each department to present this material. If this project is done, plans should be coordinated with the Sunday School superintendent and the Training Union director. Care should be taken to make certain each man assigned to a department knows what he is to present and the amount of time he should take.

(5) Congregational Worship

During the worship services on Sunday of the week of prayer the pastor may ask a member of the Baptist Men's unit to give a brief testimony and lead the congregation in special prayer for missions.

Some churches may devote the entire service to a mission emphasis and ask men to lead. Baptist Men should be willing and prepared to lead the congregation in a worship experience around a mission theme.

c. *Mission Support Groups*

Men may form mission support groups which have prayer for missions as one of its main thrusts. This approach is especially attractive to a group of retired men.

A mission support group emphasizing prayer should have a leader who is responsible for arranging for a place to meet and leading the group meeting.

Men who work in the same general area may wish to form a mission support group which meets for breakfast or lunch one day each week and emphasizes prayer. A small dining room may be reserved in a nearby restaurant where they can have privacy. Twenty to thirty minutes may be devoted to prayer for specific needs and persons in mission work.

d. *Family and Individual Prayer*

The ongoing work of Baptist Men should encourage men to pray daily for missions and to lead their families in prayer for missions. Slips of paper containing a mission need or the name of a missionary may be given to men at each Baptist Men's unit meeting. Each man accepting a prayer assignment may be asked to remember the need or person each day of the month.

2. THROUGH GIVING

Giving to support missions provides opportunity for men to become personally involved in missions. Giving is a result of effective mission study, involvement in missions, and meaningful prayer for missions. When men become informed about mission needs and engage in prayer for missions, their interest in supporting missions increases. Giving provides a way for men to express their concern.

Missions receive financial support (1) through the Cooperative Program and (2) through special offerings.

The Cooperative Program is the main stream of support to all Southern Baptist causes. This is the equitable way to meet mission needs. It needs to occupy first priority in promotion by conventions and churches.

A special offering provides opportunity for individuals to give over and above their customary tithe and offering to an area of missions in which they have special interest. It is a way for an individual Christian to express his love and gratitude to God.

The role of a Baptist Men's unit is to help the church in both means of supporting world missions. Therefore, it is imperative that all giving activities of a Baptist Men's unit be correlated with the church's plan for financial support of missions. Collecting money for a mission project separate from the church's plan will not serve the best interest of Baptist Men or world missions in the long run.

Here are some suggestions for involving men in giving:

a. *Through the Cooperative Program*

The Cooperative Program was born May 12, 1925, at the annual meeting of the Southern Baptist Convention at Memphis, Tennessee, when 34 pastors and laymen and five women affixed their signatures to a report of the Commission on Future Program, which called for a recommendation "that from the adoption of this report by the Convention, our cooperative work be known as the Cooperative Program of Southern Baptists."

The Cooperative Program was born in a time of crisis. The Seventy-Five Million Dollar Campaign had raised the sights of Southern Baptists for missionary activity at home and around the world. Daring plans had been made for advance. Financial reversal because of the economic adjustments of a post World War I panic had brought state and convention-wide agencies face to face with distressing debts.

Agencies raised money by sending special agents to the churches. This approach proved ineffective and wasteful. Members of Baptist churches were being buffeted by appeals from a different agency almost every week. Pastors and members felt frustrated. Something had to be done. The Cooperative Program was the answer.

The Cooperative Program is not a plan to be used by the agencies of any convention to raise money for their own work. The agencies do not exist for themselves. The Cooperative Program is a channel through which members in the churches respond to the commission God has given to Christians to share the good news even unto the ends of the earth.

The Cooperative Program simply is a plan of cooperation between the state conventions and the Southern Baptist Convention which makes it possible for members of churches to give to denominational causes with the assurance that the funds will be distributed on the basis of the needs and effectiveness of the programs in bringing men to God through Jesus Christ.

A Baptist Men's unit may encourage men to give through the Cooperative Program in these two ways:

(1) Ongoing Activities

The special feature period of a unit meeting is a good time to emphasize giving through the Cooperative Program. Suggestions for presentation are in *Guide*. Other ideas and information are in tracts and films, free from most state Baptist convention offices.

Some units may present the Cooperative Program in the mission study period of a unit meeting. The Mission Study Leader may wish to arrange a film or a speaker for a unit meeting. As an alternate he may use several members to make the presentation.

Printed information from books, leaflets, and tracts should be available to the men at all times. A special tract rack in an easily accessible place may be maintained for this purpose.

(2) Stewardship Projects

At some given time during the year the church may

have a special emphasis on the Cooperative Program. As part of the emphasis, Baptist Men's units may be asked to conduct a stewardship project designed to increase the church's giving through the Cooperative Program.

One such project may be to furnish speakers to speak on the Cooperative Program during Sunday School and Training Union assemblies, a church worship service, or midweek prayer meeting. If printed information for these messages is not furnished by the church, it should be ordered from the state Baptist convention office.

Another project may be to sponsor a study course in which a book on the Cooperative Program is taught. This study may be for men only or for men and women.

b. *Through Special Offerings*

The 1925 report inaugurating the Cooperative Program suggested that special interests "should be most careful in the exercise of any privilege or right of approach to individuals for large gifts not to disturb or imperil the Cooperative Program effort. It should be borne in mind that without such caution in doing so, they are imperiling our greatest and most dependable source of income for our denominational activities and disturbing the unity and fellowship of our great denomination."

Messengers to the Southern Baptist Convention recognized the wisdom of this suggestion and wrote into Section VI of their Business and Financial Plan the following: "Any special financial campaign by an agency for budget needs, endowment, building, equipment, or other purposes shall first receive the endorsement and approval of the Convention or of its Executive Committee. Neither shall any agency approach individuals or groups for special solicitation on behalf of the agency without approval of the Convention or its

Executive Committee. This does not apply to the Lottie Moon Christmas Offering or Annie Armstrong Easter Offering, nor is it to be construed as prohibiting any agency from approaching individuals for gifts for capital needs including endowments, and such approach to an individual is to be made only by personal contact or personal correspondence."

Special mission offerings have made possible the expansion of work by the Foreign Mission Board and the Home Mission Board. Both of these boards, however, look to the Cooperative Program for their basic operation and expansion needs. The Southern Baptist Convention has always recognized the right of any individual or church to designate funds.

Most churches receive special offerings for foreign, home, and state missions. In some associations, churches receive a special offering for associational missions.

The Lottie Moon Christmas Offering for Foreign Missions and the Annie Armstrong Easter Offering for Home Missions were originally promoted by the Woman's Missionary Union alone. Increasingly, these special offerings became church offerings with the Woman's Missionary Union and Brotherhood sharing in their planning and promotion.

State mission offering dates and promotional methods are determined by each individual state.

A Baptist Men's unit engages in the promotion of special offerings on assignment from the church. Its goal may be a part of the church goal. In churches which use this plan, Baptist Men's units should encourage men to consider the following responsibilities:

- Make certain at least a tithe of the family income is given through the church budget.
- Encourage the church to give liberally to missions through the Cooperative Program.

- Encourage the church to set special offering goals commensurate with the membership's giving potential.
- Lead each member of the family to understand the purpose of the special offerings for home and foreign missions and their significance.
- See that each member of the family contributes individually to the special offerings.
- Lead children to understand that giving money is not a substitute for giving their lives to mission service.

If the churches do not have a special offering for foreign missions, the Baptist Men's unit should provide the opportunity for men to give. Leaders will want to emphasize the spiritual values accruing from such an offering and guard against it becoming merely a money-raising campaign.

c. *Through Mission Support Groups*

Mission support groups may perform activities which lead men to support missions financially. Under the direction of the Mission Activity Leader, the mission support group leader may direct projects which encourage men to increase their giving through the church to special mission offerings and the Cooperative Program.

B. PROVIDING AND INTERPRETING INFORMATION

All church members need to be informed about the work of their church and denomination. All church program organizations share a common task in communicating this information. A Baptist Men's unit mainly uses its ongoing activities to accomplish this task.

The performance of this task should result in more men participating meaningfully in the life and work of the church and denomination (association, state, convention, and Southern Baptist Convention).

1. SECURING INFORMATION

a. *From the Church*

Information about the church's program may come from the Brotherhood director, the minister of education, and the pastor. The president of Baptist Men should be alert to all announcements printed in the church paper and bulletin. Communicating information about the more complex church programs will require study of all details.

b. *From the Denomination*

Information may be obtained from mission magazines, state Baptist papers, and correspondence from the association, state Baptist convention and Southern Baptist Convention agencies.

2. COMMUNICATING INFORMATION

a. *Unit Meetings*

The opening period of each unit meeting is the best time to provide information about the church and denomination to members of a Baptist Men's unit. The president or other men designated by him may present the information. Other announcements about church, associational, and state meetings may be made at this time.

Attractive posters on emphases and other future events should be displayed in conspicuous places during a unit meeting.

Tracts, leaflets, and other items containing information may be distributed to the members during a unit meeting.

Occasionally but not frequently the unit may devote the mission study period to sharing information about a very significant church or denominational activity, using projected visuals or a speaker.

b. *Projects*

A church may ask its Baptist Men's unit to engage in a special project to communicate information. Examples are distributing leaflets to home, erecting signs, and making announcements in assemblies of Sunday School and Training Union.

C. CONDUCTING SPECIAL PROJECTS

Although Baptist Men do not have an exclusive task of providing leaders and organization for special projects of the church, traditionally many churches make a practice of calling on its Baptist Men's units for this service. Therefore, a unit needs to be prepared to fulfill these requests. While there are many church projects, here are three of the best known ones a church may ask units to perform:

1. SUPPORTING REVIVAL MEETINGS

A revival is a special project of the church which normally requires the resources of all organizations. During a church revival, the Sunday School should lead all church members to witness and to invite all prospects to attend.

However, the church usually asks the Baptist Men's units to sponsor some special projects to support the revival meeting. They are:

a. *Neighborhood Prayer Meetings*

The church may assign to the Baptist Men's unit the responsibility of planning and conducting neighborhood prayer meetings at several locations in the community. The following suggestions may be helpful in guiding, planning, and conducting these prayer meetings.

(1) Planning

Effective neighborhood prayer meetings are the result of much thought, prayer, planning, and other serious efforts. Preparation should begin many months before the opening date of a revival.

First, a committee should be appointed. The Baptist Men's president may ask the Mission Activity Leader to serve as chairman of the committee. An alternative is to ask another man to take charge of the committee under the general supervision of the Mission Activity Leader. The chairman and the members of the committee should consider this process:

(a) Set the Dates.

Experience has proven that the best time to hold neighborhood prayer meetings is during the week preceding the revival. The usual procedure is to conduct the prayer meetings on Monday, Tuesday, Thursday and Friday nights. Several different locations may be selected for prayer meetings on each of these nights. For example, if eight meetings are scheduled, two may be held on Monday, two on Tuesday, two on Thursday, and two on Friday.

(b) Set the Time

Neighborhood prayer meetings should last about one hour. An additional half hour may be used for visitation. Here is a suggested schedule:

7:30–8:30—Neighborhood prayer meetings
8:30–9:00—Visitation of unsaved persons or unaffiliated Baptists

(c) Determine Number

The number of neighborhood prayer meetings will depend upon the size of church membership, qualified leaders available, and number of homes which may be secured for the prayer meetings. In most churches one prayer meeting is held for each 25 resident members.

(d) Secure Meeting Places

Prayer meetings should be held in various sections of the community where the church members live. Leaders should place meeting places as strategically as possible, getting permission to hold the meeting well in advance. At the same time, they need to tell each host the date, the time of the meeting, who will lead the service, and how many persons may attend.

(e) Choose the Leadership

Choosing leaders of the prayer services well ahead of the meetings permits the committee to instruct the chosen persons well. If possible, the leaders should not select as a prayer leader the person in whose home the prayer meeting is scheduled.

Leadership teams should consist of a leader to preside at the meeting, a song leader, and someone to help the host get chairs, song books, and other equipment.

(f) Instruct the Leadership Teams

The committee should arrange a meeting of the leadership teams about one month before the neighborhood prayer meetings to discuss plans, complete the agenda, and make sure each person understands what he is to do. Suggested agenda items include:

- Completing agenda for prayer meeting

- Arranging for leaders to arrive early to greet and introduce persons as they arrive
- Lighting homes for easy identification
- Arranging for hymn books and the appropriate use of hymns
- Having as many people as possible read assigned Scripture passages, and giving brief testimonies
- Interspersing periods of prayer
- Providing opportunities for taking prayer requests
- Studying methods for inviting neighbors to attend the prayer meeting
- Learning how to conduct the soul-winning visitation following the prayer meeting
- Getting the names of the unsaved and the unaffiliated for use at the prayer meeting.

(g) Inform the Church Membership

The entire church membership should be invited verbally or by mail to attend the prayer meetings. If mail is used, the letter should mention the date and time of all meetings, the name of the host and hostess with addresses of homes in which the meetings are to be held, and the hope all members will attend the most convenient session.

Other advertising media include the church bulletin, announcements from the pulpit, announcements in the Sunday School and Training Union assemblies, and articles in local newspapers.

(2) Conducting the Prayer Meetings

Each leadership team should prepare an agenda for the prayer meeting. The agenda should include the use of prayer hymns, a brief statement of the purpose of the meeting made by the leader, Scripture reading, and maximum opportunity for everyone to pray.

Specific objects of prayer may be the pastor, the evangelist, song leader, the choir, the instrumentalists, and others who will assist in the revival. Pray specifically for those who need to be reached for Christ through the revival meeting.

Individual testimonies of answered prayer or soul-winning experiences may be a part of the agenda.

At the close of the meeting, the names and addresses of the unsaved should be made available to those planning to visit.

b. *Prayer Breakfast*

The prayer breakfast should be well planned and simple. There should be time for at least one hymn and Scripture reading at the beginning. The person presiding should give individuals an opportunity to mention special prayer requests, including the names of unsaved persons to whom they will be witnessing. Announcements should be kept to a minimum.

Sometimes men bring their unsaved friends to a prayer breakfast. These men should be recognized as visitors and made to feel welcome.

A season of prayer should be the major emphasis. It is not necessary to have a speaker. If the visiting evangelist is present, the person presiding may present him to the men and give him an opportunity to express briefly his expectations for the week.

It is unwise to use the prayer breakfast as a promotional device. This is a time when men who are already Christians should be seeking the leadership of the Holy Spirit and committing anew their lives for service.

c. *Visitation*

Men should be enlisted to visit prospects before and during the revival meeting. Some churches ask Baptist Men's units to furnish the leadership for planning and promoting visitation. Other churches use the Sunday School organization for this purpose. In either case, the Baptist Men's unit will want to involve as many men as possible.

A list of prospects should be prepared from which visitation assignments may be made. The most accessible of the unchurched people in the community will already be on the Sunday School roll. Names are available from a recent religious census or community census. Cards containing the names of prospects can be distributed among the men at the Baptist Men's meeting prior to the revival meeting.

d. *Transportation*

The church may need to furnish transportation for some persons who desire to attend the revival meeting. The Baptist Men's unit can help meet this need.

In planning to furnish transportation, at least three questions must be answered: (1) Who needs transportation? (2) How many automobiles and drivers are available? (3) How can those who need transportation be made aware that it is available?

The Baptist Men's unit will need to conduct a survey of the community to find those who need transportation. Special planning to enlist drivers is also essential.

Names and addresses of persons needing transportation should be given to each driver. The driver should contact all persons assigned to him and agree on the time he will pick them up.

Several extra drivers and automobiles should be enlisted for this project. If one of the drivers is unable to meet his responsibility, a substitute should be called.

2. STARTING A CHURCH TYPE MISSION

Organizing a mission is a man-size job. Every Baptist Men's unit should take this task seriously and be ready to help the church in any way possible in such an undertaking.

Before beginning this work, the officers of the Baptist Men's unit should ask themselves these questions:

Has an honest effort been made by our church to determine the need for a mission?

Has the Baptist Men's unit diligently participated in this effort?

If the idea for beginning a mission originates with the planning committee of the Baptist Men's unit, the project should be discussed with the pastor, the Brotherhood director, the associational superintendent of missions, and the missions committees of the association and church.

With the help of the church missions committee and the associational missions committee, a decision should be reached on the location and type of new work to be started.

As many men as possible should be enlisted to help take a religious survey of the area, to visit, and to help prepare the building for the meeting.

If a mission Sunday School is started, men should be encouraged to serve as teachers and officers.

A layman-sponsored revival preceding or following the beginning of a mission needs to be planned carefully. The building selected for the meeting should be centrally located and free of distractions.

A spirit of good will must be established between the laymen's team and the residents of the community where the new work is to be established. This good can be accomplished by visiting in homes prior to the revival and involving these people in planning and conducting the services.

3. STEWARDSHIP CAMPAIGNS

The Stewardship Commission of the Southern Baptist Convention and offices of state Baptist conventions provide excellent guidance for churches in stewardship campaigns. Since approaches vary in each campaign a Baptist Men's unit should follow the suggestions of the campaign director when helping with this special project.

4. OTHER MISSION ASSISTANCE

Periodically, Southern Baptists in sections of the nation where organized Southern Baptist work is weak issue pleas for help through the Home Mission Board. Through special projects of the church Baptist Men's units reply to these pleas with offers of manpower. Sometimes the need is for men to take surveys. Other times it's to witness as part of a large evangelistic effort.

This work is assigned to a special projects leader by the Mission Activity Leader once the project is approved by the church.

6. *Enlisting Men and Reporting Progress*

CHAPTER OUTLINE

A. ENLISTMENT AND ADVERTISING

1. MEMBERSHIP
2. PROSPECTS
3. FACTORS INFLUENCING ENLISTMENT

B. RECORDS AND REPORTS

1. THE RECORD AND REPORT SYSTEM
2. MAKING REPORTS LIVE

● All of the content and methods for involving men in learning experiences are of little value unless men are enlisted in a mission program which helps them live a little better as Christians each day. Enlistment and records play distinct roles in a mission program for men.

The vice-president and secretary of a Baptist Men's unit determine the success or failure of the unit because of their close relationship to enlistment and records. The vice-president is primarily responsible for promoting attendance and increasing enrollment. The secretary is responsible for recording and reporting the participation of members. Together, they provide the backdrop for evaluating how effective the mission program is.

A. ENLISTMENT AND ADVERTISING

1. MEMBERSHIP

A man may become a member of a Baptist Men's unit by participating in an organized activity of a unit and filling out an enrollment card.

An organized activity is a meeting or activity planned and directed by the men of a Baptist Men's unit.

2. PROSPECTS

The first step in enlisting men is to determine the prospects for membership in a Baptist Men's unit. If a church has only one unit, all men in the church 18 years old and above are prospects. In churches with more than one unit the Brotherhood council determine the prospects for each unit.

The vice-president should take the initiative to determine who the prospects are. Here are some suggestions.

● Secure from the church office or church clerk a list

of names and addresses of all men on the church roll.

- If the church has more than one Baptist Men's unit, ask the Brotherhood council to indicate who are prospects for the units.
- Compare the list of prospects with the names of men already enrolled in a unit.
- Contact each prospect and invite him to attend the unit meeting.

3. FACTORS INFLUENCING ENLISTMENT

There are eight factors which influence the effectiveness of an enlistment program. Some of these factors are not the direct responsibility of the vice-president, however, he needs to permit them to influence the work of the unit.

a. *Know the Unit's Work and Purpose*

The more a salesman knows about his product the easier it is for him to sell it. Persons who seek to enlist men for a Baptist Men's unit must know the concepts on which it is based and the work it is designed to perform. Therefore, it is essential that the vice-president, as well as other officers, know all of the content of this book.

b. *Understand the Needs of Men*

The needs of men which can be effectively met by a Baptist Men's unit may vary from church to church. Nevertheless, there are some basic needs common to all Baptist men. Persons responsible for enlistment should study the men to determine their specific needs and make enlistment plans which appeal to them. Here are some basic needs of men:

- Men need to grow in their understanding of the church's mission.

- Men need to discover God's plan for their individual lives.
- Men need fellowship with other Christian men.
- Men need to engage in activities which they feel are meaningful ways to serve God.

c. *Provide Informative and Interesting Meetings*

One of the most important assets to an enlistment plan is informative and interesting unit meetings. It is difficult for a promotional plan to overcome the mental block caused by the memory of a poorly-planned and conducted meeting. Every unit meeting should present information to men in an interesting way. Those leaders responsible for planning and conducting unit meetings should try to make every meeting of such quality the men feel it worthy of the time and effort required for them to attend.

d. *Provide Worthy Activities*

Men soon grow tired of a meeting which is an end within itself. Every meeting should point the way to worthwhile activities. Men can be challenged to act if they understand the need for the action. A unit without activities is dead.

e. *Provide Wholesome Atmosphere in Unit Meetings*

Leaders are responsible for the atmosphere of a meeting. For example, a president who constantly reminds the unit that only 50 men are in attendance when he expected 100 generates the atmosphere of defeat. On the other hand, a few cheerful greetings and hearty handshakes before a well planned and conducted program will cause an atmosphere of friendliness and optimism to prevail.

Things which build atmosphere into a unit meeting are

both physical and personal. The arrangements of furniture such as chairs, table, and speaker's stand can influence the atmosphere. The seating arrangement should permit each person to see all who are in attendance, including the speaker when he addresses the group.

Perhaps the most important single factor in creating the right atmosphere is to express a sincere interest in each member. Persons should be stationed at all entrances to the meeting room. These persons should greet men as they arrive and see that each one finds someone with whom he may talk until the meeting begins. Names of all visitors and prospective members should be noted. A list of these names should be handed to the vice-president before the meeting begins so he can present them to the unit.

f. *Recognize Visitors and New Members*

The vice-president should recognize all visitors and new members during the unit meeting. He may ask different members to present the visitors and new members. Some units present new members a Baptist Men's lapel button. The president may wish to talk briefly about the responsibility of membership.

g. *Involve New Members Promptly*

Each new member should be asked to fill out an enrollment card and offered an opportunity to join a mission action group as soon as possible. By the next unit meeting he should get an assignment. He may become a member of the welcoming committee or table serving group, or present visitors and new members.

h. *Publicize Meetings and Activities*

Attractive advertising is essential to enlistment. This concept covers more than announcements in Sunday School classes and worship services. It calls for posters in prominent places, postal cards, letters, telephone cards, and personal contacts.

(1) Link Publicity to Desires of Men

Each means of advertising meetings and activities should be used to motivate men to participate. A person preparing announcements should know the basic desires of Baptist men and seek to appeal to them. Some basic desires are for:

- Knowledge
- Improvement of skills
- Feeling needed
- Fellowship.

(2) Put Advertising Message on High Plane

Every announcement about a meeting should tell six things in an attractive way. They are who, what, when, where, why and how.

In many respects the message of the advertising piece may determine the success of a meeting. If the appeal is based on food, fun, and fellowship alone, the men may not recognize the highest qualities of a meeting such as information and the challenge of service. The message in advertising should convey the spirit, content, and benefits of the meeting or activity being promoted.

(3) Use Variety of Methods

Here are eight good methods for publicizing meetings and activities. The vice-president will want to vary their use to maintain a fresh approach to the men.

(a) Bulletin Boards

A special Baptist Men's bulletin board may be erected

at a prominent place in the church. In large churches more than one bulletin board will be needed. Bulletin boards should be located in places frequented by men. The vice-president should see that old announcements are removed and new announcements are placed on the board. The board should always contain some message.

(b) Posters

Posters are easy to make and are effective for promotion. The vice-president may ask a member who has artistic ability to prepare a poster each month.

Immediately following a unit meeting the old poster should be replaced by a new poster advertising the next meeting. Other than the value of promoting attendance, an attractive poster will remind all church members that the church has a mission program for men.

(c) Post Cards and Letters

Post cards and letters can be used effectively to promote attendance. They should contain a brief message including the name of the unit, time and date of the meeting, program topic, speakers, and a word on the value of the meeting for men. Cards and letters should be mailed at least one week before the meeting.

(d) Telephone Calls

The telephone is not the best promotional tool, however, it may be used as a means of following up announcements, cards and letters and to get final commitments to attend or perform a responsibility at the meeting. The names of unit members and prospects may be divided among the officers. Each member and prospect should be called a few days before the meeting.

(e) Personal Contact

No promotional method is more effective than personal contacts. Process for using this method is to assign each officer the names of members and prospects to contact. These contacts may be made at other church meetings, on the job, or in the homes. A friendly handshake and a warm invitation are good incentives for a man to attend the meeting.

(f) Newsletters and Bulletins

The church newsletter and bulletin should always carry a brief statement or announcement about the unit's work and meetings. As in all forms of announcements the message should be clearly stated and brief.

(g) Articles in Local Newspapers

Many local newspapers will gladly carry announcements about church meetings. Before asking an editor to print an article, someone familiar with news writing should read the article. Sometimes the editor will help reword the article to convey the same message and consume less space.

(h) Radio and Television Announcements

If a local radio or television station has community interest time in their programming plan, the Baptist Men's unit may use this means to advertise meetings and activities. Usually it is best to save radio and television for advertising such occasions as Baptist Men's Day and other special events.

B. RECORDS AND REPORTS

Essential to reporting progress are accurate records and meaningful reports. The records of unit activities indicate the degree of progress the unit has made toward its objective and goals. Reports provide a systematic way of communicating to the unit, Brotherhood, and church the work completed by a unit. Together, records and reports provide the information necessary for evaluating a unit's work.

Usually a unit keeps records of men's involvement in mission study, mission activities such as mission action, organized prayer activities, special giving activities, and projects and finances. These records provide information which is summarized and reported on special forms in the unit's record and report system.

1. THE RECORD AND REPORT SYSTEM

The record and report system is composed of enrollment cards for the members and *Baptist Men's Record and Report,* a looseleaf book for the secretary to use in keeping records and making reports. In addition to the secretary's section the book has four sections for use by the Mission Activity Leader, Mission Study Leader, mission action group leaders and working group leaders in helping the secretary compile his records. Each section contains instructions for using the section, a directory, forms for keeping permanent records, and forms for making 12 monthly reports. The enrollment cards and *Baptist Men's Record and Report* are sold at the Baptist book store. A special three ring binder with the Baptist Men's emblem is available from Baptist book stores for holding this book.

a. *Enrollment Card*

An enrollment card is completed by each member at the time he joins a unit. It is filed by the secretary for use by officers when forming working groups and promoting attendance.

b. *Baptist Men's Record and Report Book*

(1) Secretary's Record and Report Section

This section is used by the secretary to record attendance at unit meetings and to compile the information on the monthly reports from the Mission Study Leader and Mission Activity Leader.

```
┌──────────────────────────────────────────────────────────────┐
│                    ┌─────────────┐                            │
│                    │ Baptist Men │         Enrollment Card    │
│                    └─────────────┘                            │
│  Unit_____│
│  ═════════════════════════════════════════════════════════   │
│                                                               │
│  Name _____   Off. Phone _____ │
│                                                               │
│  Address _____   Res. Phone _____ │
│                                                               │
│  City _____   State _____ │
│                                                               │
│  Occupation _____   Bus. Address _____ │
│  ═════════════════════════════════════════════════════════   │
│                                                               │
│  I am interested in participating in Baptist Men's:           │
│                                                               │
│  Mission Study Groups .............. ____   Mission Support Groups ............. ____ │
│  Mission Action Groups ............. ____   Mission Action Projects ........... ____ │
│  Mission Action Surveys ............ ____   Church Projects ................... ____ │
│                              (over)                           │
└──────────────────────────────────────────────────────────────┘
```

Each month the secretary fills out two report forms, one for the president and the other for the central record of the church. The president shares his report with the Brotherhood director. The secretary may give a copy of the unit report to the church clerk in churches without a central record office.

A unit's monthly report to the Brotherhood, along with reports from other units, becomes part of the Brotherhood director's report to the church. Churches which have no Brotherhood director may ask the Baptist Men's president to report to the church.

The secretary also needs to keep minutes of planning meetings and unit meetings and records of finances. Forms are provided for these purposes.

Minutes of planning meetings and unit meetings should contain the important actions approved by the group. A detailed account of activities at meetings is unnecessary.

An accurate record of all funds received by the unit and an itemized account of their use should be kept.

A report of receipts and disbursements should be made regularly to the Brotherhood council or to the church if there is no Brotherhood council.

(2) Mission Study Leader's Record and Report Section

This section is used by the Mission Study Leader to record and report the participation of members of the unit in group and individual mission studies. The number of men participating in group study is obtained by a head count during special group mission studies and from reports by mission study group leaders. The number of men participating in individual study is determined by individual reports to the Mission Study Leader by men who complete the study of a mission book. Usually the Mission Study Leader keeps informed of the individual study underway by giving mission books to individual men and asking them to inform him when they complete the book.

Each month the Mission Study Leader completes a report form for the unit secretary.

(3) Mission Activity Leader's Record and Report Section

This section is used by the Mission Activity Leader to record and report participation of members of the unit in the activities of mission action groups, mission projects which are not part of a group's activities. Support activities, and special projects. Information on participation in activities is obtained from monthly reports of mission action group leaders and working group leaders.

Each month the Mission Activity Leader completes a report form for the unit secretary.

(4) Mission Action Group Leader's Records and Reports Section

This section is used by each mission action group leader to record and report the participation of members of his group in meetings and actions. Information is obtained by head count at each meeting or action.

Group meetings are meetings the group holds to plan, evaluate, share, and train.

Actions are the activities performed by the group in serving the persons toward whom the ministry is directed.

Each month this leader completes a report form for the Mission Activity Leader.

(5) Working Group Leaders' Record and Report Section

This section is used by working group leaders, other than mission action group leaders, to record and report the participation of men in any small group activities conducted by Baptist Men other than mission action. The number participating is determined by head count during each activity.

Examples of working groups are: mission study groups (page 60), mission action projects not directed by a mission action group (pages 77-79), mission support groups (pages 90-91), and special project groups (page 98-105).

Each month mission study group leaders complete a report for the Mission Study Leader. All other working group leaders complete a monthly report for the Mission Activity Leader.

2. MAKING REPORTS LIVE

Few things are more essential than statistics for progress reports, and nothing more boring than statistics alone. The persons making reports should recognize the need for additional information which adds life to reports. Here are some suggestions which may brighten Baptist Men's reports:

- Human interest accounts such as results from mission action
- Brief description of needs of people served by mission action groups
- Quotes from persons who express appreciation for service

- Occasional touch of humor in good taste
- Comparison of statistics with achievement possibilities
- Recognition of individuals or groups providing outstanding service
- Brief statement on future plans
- Expression of gratitude to church or individual church leaders for special provisions made in the interest of work to be done by the unit.

Personal Learning Activities

CHAPTER I

1. What is the object of Baptist Men?
2. List the four tasks normally assigned to Brotherhood.
3. What three factors influence the number of Baptist Men's units a church may have?
4. How are working groups formed?

CHAPTER II

1. How is the planning committee formed?
2. List four factors which contribute to effective planning.
3. How often should the planning committee meet?
4. How is the work of a Baptist Men's unit financed?

CHAPTER III

1. What are three major areas of content of mission study?
2. List three ways a Baptist Men's unit provides mission study opportunities.
3. What are three mission study or learning methods?
4. How does a panel differ from a symposium?

CHAPTER IV

1. What are the two types of surveys a church may use to discover mission action needs?

2. What is the difference between on-going actions and projects?

3. List five steps for beginning on-going actions.

4. When are joint mission action groups formed?

CHAPTER V

1. List three ways a Baptist Men's unit helps the church enlarge its mission support.

2. Give two sources of information to be communicated to members of a Baptist Men's unit.

3. What are two ways missions receive financial support?

4. List four ways a Baptist Men's unit can assist with a church revival.

CHAPTER VI

1. How does a man become a member of a Baptist Men's unit?

2. What are five ways to advertise a meeting?

3. To whom does the president of a Baptist Men's unit make his monthly report?

4. Of the three suggested working groups, which one has a record and report booklet?

Requirements for Credit

● This book is the text for course number 6602 in the Christian Leadership Series, Church Study Course.

Persons can earn credit for this book the following ways in these amounts:

Event	Credits	
Class study for 2½ hours	1	
Class study for 5 hours	2	
Individual study (completing questions, exercises)	2	
Reading only	1	
Educational institution plan	4	
SBC, state assemblies, seminars, workshops	1	(each 2½ hours of class time)

If credit is desired for this course through class study, individual study, or by reading, the following requirements must be met:

I. CLASSWORK

1. The class must meet a minimum of five hours. The required time does not include laboratory experience or practice. For courses in which laboratory experience or practice is desirable, two hours of such guided experience

may be substituted as one hour of class time, provided at least half of the required hours are actually spent in class-work.

2. A class member who attends all class sessions and completes the reading of the book as directed by the teacher will not be required to do any written work for credit.

3. A class member who is absent from one or more sessions must complete the required exercises or questions in the "Personal Learning Activities" section on all chapters he misses. In such a case, he must turn in his paper by the date the teacher sets (usually within ten days following the last class). Also, he must certify that he has read the book.

4. The teacher should request an award for himself. A person who teaches a course for Youth or Adults (in any subject area) will be granted the same number of credits as class members. Request award by using Form 151.

5. The director of church training should complete the "Request for Course Credit" (Form 151) and forward it after completion of the class to the Church Study Course Awards Office, 127 Ninth Avenue, North, Nashville, Tennessee 37203.

II. INDIVIDUAL STUDY

1. A person who wishes to complete this course without attending class sessions may receive full credit by certifying he has read the book and completing all exercises or questions in the "Personal Learning Activities" section.

2. Students may find profit in studying the text together, but individual papers are required. Carbon copies or duplicates of the answers cannot be accepted.

3. The work required for individual study credit should be turned in for checking to the director of church training or

the person designated by the church to administer the Christian Leadership Series. The form entitled "Request for Course Credit" (Form 151) must be used in requesting these awards. It is to be forwarded by the director of church training or the person designated by the church to the Church Study Course Awards Office, 127 Ninth Avenue, North, Nashville, Tennessee 37203.

III. READING CREDIT

1. A person may receive one credit toward the certificates (or diploma) on which he is working by simply reading this book.

2. Upon completion of the reading, he must complete "Request for Reading Credit" (Form 151). He should give the completed form to the director of church training, or the person designated by his church to be responsible for administering the Christian Leadership Series.

3. The director of church training or the person designated by the church will see that the request is completed, signed, and forwarded to the Church Study Course Awards Office, 127 Ninth Avenue, North, Nashville, Tennessee 37203.

IV. AWARDS AND RECORDS

Two copies of the course credit award form will be sent by the Study Course Awards Office to the church. One copy should be filed in the church training record and the other given to the individual.